WIT

Ethnic Groups and Marital Choices

Since the late nineteenth century, the rate of intermarriage between members of different European ethnic and cultural groups in Canada has increased and resulted in a gradual blending of these communities. Using data from the 1871 Census of Canada, Madeline Richard makes the first estimates of the extent of intermarriage in Canada in 1871, providing insights as to which ethnic groups intermarried and with whom, and as to what the correlates of intermarriage were at the time. The same estimates are made for 1971, utilizing data from the 1971 Census, which allows for a unique comparison between rates, patterns, and correlates of intermarriage in nineteenth- and twentieth-century Canada.

In addition to delineating general patterns of intermarriage, as well as trends for the English, Irish, Scottish, French, and Germans, this study determines the effects of a husband's level of literacy, nativity, age, and place of residence on the odds of marrying outside his ethno-religious origin, and the effect of an ethic group's socio-demographic characteristics on the propensity to marry exogamously. Richard's findings confirm that marital assimilation was occurring in Canada to some extent as early as 1871 and that the rate of intermarriage has doubled since then.

This book is not only about marital patterns; it is also about the ethnic groups themselves. Detailed descriptions of the English, Irish, Scottish, French, German, Italian, Dutch, Polish, Scandinavian, Ukrainian, and other groups are given, including their immigration history, settlement patterns, and socio-demographic characteristics, all of which have some bearing on patterns of mate selection.

The first detailed comparative study of ethno-religious intermarriage, *Ethnic Groups and Marital Choices* illuminates our understanding of the dynamics of intermarriage in a culturally pluralistic society such as Canada.

MADELINE A. RICHARD is acting director of the Population Research Laboratory at Erindale College, University of Toronto.

HQ1031R53Y91

ETHNIC GROUPS AND MARI

RICHARD MADELINE

MADELINE A. RICHARD

Ethnic Groups and Marital Choices

Ethnic History and Marital Assimilation in Canada, 1871 and 1971

UBCPress
Vancouver

© UBC Press 1991

Reprinted 1992

All rights reserved

Printed in Canada on acid-free paper ∞

ISBN 0-7748-0431-9

Canadian Cataloguing in Publication Data

Richard, Madeline A.

Ethnic groups and marital choices

Includes bibliographical references and index.

ISBN 0-7748-0431-9

1. Intermarriage - Canada. 2. Canada -
Population - Ethnic groups. 3. Assimilation
(Sociology). I. Title.

HQ1031.R53 1991   306.84'5'0971   C91-091143-6

This book has been published with the help of a grant
from the Social Science Federation of Canada, using funds
provided by the Social Sciences and Humanities Research
Council of Canada.

UBC Press
University of British Columbia
6344 Memorial Rd
Vancouver, BC V6T 1Z2
(604) 822-3259
Fax: (604) 822-6083

Printed and bound in Canada
by John Deyell Company

For Warren E. Kalbach

Contents

PP 6-40 only

Tables and Figures

TABLES

FIGURES

Acknowledgments

This book would not have been possible without the support of Gordon Darroch of York University. He provided me with the Canadian Historical Mobility Project data, supported and encouraged my work, and made many useful comments and suggestions on this draft.

I am also indebted to Jim Moore and Jean Burnet. Ann Sorenson and Olga Fraser provided valuable consultation on statistical matters. Margaret Currie and Elaine Goettler made the 1871 Census volumes and other reference material readily available. Joe Lim provided valuable technical assistance and expertise on computer equipment and software. Kim Hall, Luke Pereira, Dawn Scovell, and Sherrilyn Sklar provided excellent research assistance.

My gratitude is also extended to my parents, Ernest and Olive Bridger, and to my children Catharine and Michael. Their support has been appreciated.

To Warren E. Kalbach, my husband and colleague, I express my gratitude for a deep and lasting influence. This is for him.

ETHNIC GROUPS AND MARITAL CHOICES

Introduction

Assimilation has been a major concern of politicians, as well as sociologists and other social scientists, since the early 1900s. Woodsworth, for example, stated that 'we in Canada, have certain more or less clearly defined ideals of national well-being' and that 'these ideals must never be lost sight of. Non-ideal elements there must be, but they should be capable of assimilation' (1909:278). During the 1960s and 1970s, however, there seemed to be a greater awareness of, and a concern for, ethnic survival throughout the world. Americans referred to it as an 'ethnic revival,' but in Canada it was seen 'primarily as a cultural movement' (Reitz 1980:44). The government's policy of multiculturalism, 'which is regarded as an expression of a desire to respect and preserve ethnic heritage for its own sake' (ibid.), is a case in point. However, the programs announced had as much to do with removing barriers to full participation in Canadian society and with inter-cultural activity, and therefore with assimilation, as it did with the preservation of ethnic heritages. There is, it seems, a basic contradiction between the name given to the policy, that is, multiculturalism, and what in fact happens. As Burnet (1987) points out, the maintenance of the many cultures in Canada is not possible. Moreover, no ethnic or cultural group can maintain all that it brings to a new land, but 'it is ethnic identity that can and does persist, and selected cultural patterns as symbolic expression of that identity' (ibid.: 70).

This renewed interest in ethnicity has brought the inevitability and necessity for assimilation into question, especially by ethnic groups themselves, but the dominant fact of life remains one of social mobility and socio-economic assimilation into the large institutional structures of Canadian society. It is true that immigrants bring with them their own distinct cultural and ethnic heritage along with a desire to preserve their customs in the new land. While they tend to seek the familiar and comfortable in their new home-land, they are also motivated to change their attitudes and mode of life in order to achieve social and economic success. Immigrants may seek new employment opportunities and more education and im-prove their language and occupational skills. To facilitate assimila-tion and integration in their new society they can join new organizations, meet new friends, and, if single, marry someone from the dominant group. Of the many pathways to social and economic integration intermarriage is considered central.

SCOPE OF THE STUDY

This book is not just about ethnic pattens of marital choices. It is also about the ethnic groups themselves. Data are presented for the English, Irish, Scottish, French, German, Italian, Dutch, Polish, Scandinavian, Ukrainian, and 'Other' groups. All these groups were here in sufficient numbers at the time of the 1871 Census (except the Ukrainians) to be reported in that census. The details of their immigration history, settlement patterns, and socio-demographic characteristics are given some prominence because all had some bearing on their patterns of mate selection. Thus considerable attention has been given to these factors. Although the treatment of each ethnic group is far from complete and is variable in length, an attempt has been made to provide as much of the historical informa-tion as possible to facilitate an understanding of patterns of marital choices in Canada in 1871 and 1971. In so doing, this research goes beyond the current knowledge of patterns of intermarriage and correlates through the addition of new research findings arising from the use of data that were previously unavailable to researchers, namely, the 1871 Census of Canada. It also marks the first time that a detailed comparative analysis of ethno-religious intermarriage has been undertaken.

This book answers three major questions about marital assimila-tion, and, in so doing, demonstrates the usefulness of intermarriage both as a measure and as an indicator of assimilation. The first question centres around not whether marital assimilation occurred, but to what extent it had progressed by 1971. What were the patterns of incidence for Canada's ethnic populations? Did these patterns change over the century? What progress, from the stand-point of intermarriage with the British (or English) and the French, had been made over the century? What marital choices were made by ethnic groups? Were the same marital choices made in both centuries?

Some ethnic attributes, such as an ability to speak English, can be considered indicators of an individual's assimilation. Similarly, one can consider an ethnic group in terms of level of assimilation by examining certain attributes of the group as a whole, such as the proportion of its members able to speak English (Lieberson 1963). The second and third questions then, deal with the factors that promoted or retarded assimilation through intermarriage and differences in patterns of assimilation among ethnic groups and individuals. Were the same factors responsible in both the nineteenth and twentieth centuries? Hence, did mid-twentieth-century findings apply to the nineteenth century? If there were differences among ethnic groups, what caused these differences? Among individuals, who were the most likely to assimilate through intermarriage and thereby reduce their original ethnic-connectedness?

The objective of this work is to develop an understanding of ethno-religious intermarriage in Canada in 1871 and 1971. It is unique in using data that allow a comparison over the century. The analysis focuses on rates, patterns, and correlates for husbands because, traditionally, the husband's role has been clearly defined in terms of responsibility for the economic and social well-being of his wife and children (Kalbach and McVey 1979; Veevers 1977). Historically, women have derived their status from that of their husband, and they were not the major economic providers in husband-wife families. This is particularly true for the two time periods, 1871 and 1971. By 1971 only 34.6 per cent of women participated in the labour force, and for most ethnic groups included in this analysis, the proportion was about 21 per cent, with the exception of the French at 29.8 per cent. Hence, the labour force participation rates of immigrant women were remarkably similar and relatively low. In addition, calculation of the propensities for intermarriage based on wives indicates that wives are very similar to husbands in their marital choices. Although patterns of intermarriage and its consequences differ between sexes, assimilation has been historically defined in terms of husbands' socio-economic position. A focus on male patterns provides for an analysis of the main determinants of assimilation, but it is also recognized that these are not the only determinants. While it is acknowledged that a study of women's patterns of marital assimilation could be undertaken with these data, it is also argued that such a study would be more relevant if it focused on the decade of the 1980s.

This book consists of seven chapters. Following the introduction,

Chapter 2 examines the relationship between intermarriage and assimilation through a systematic overview of relevant research on patterns and correlates and determinants of intermarriage. In addition, it discusses various theories of assimilation as they relate to intermarriage. Chapter 3 presents the historical background necessary for a clearer understanding of ethno-religious intermarriage in Canada. More specifically, Chapter 3 deals with the individual ethnic or cultural origin groups, that is, English, Irish, Scottish, French, German, Italian, Dutch, Polish, Scandinavian, Ukrainian, and Other origin groups. A portrait of each group's immigration pattern over the century and its settlement patterns is presented. Chapter 4 examines selected characteristics of the ethnic origin groups, such as size, religious composition, nativity, age and sex distributions, occupational distribution, rural-urban character, and levels of literacy. To summarize, these three chapters cover the social, cultural, economic, and geographical contexts within which ethno-religious intermarriage took place in Canada in 1871 and 1971.

The factors examined in chapters 3 and 4 have been shown either to facilitate or to limit intermarriage in the twentieth century. The question is whether they had the same effect in nineteenth-century Canada. Chapters 5 and 6 compare the prevalence, patterns, and correlates of ethnic and ethno-religious intermarriage in nineteenth- and twentieth-century Canada, specifically for 1871 and 1971. Chapter 5 concentrates on patterns of ethnic and ethno-religious inter-marriage in terms of percentages and propensities. Chapter 6 determines the association, as measured by Spearman's rank order correlation coefficient, between the propensities of husbands to outmarry and selected group socio-demographic characteristics, that is, per cent urban, per cent native born, per cent belonging to the ethnic church, population size, age, sex ratio (males per one hundred females), occupational status, and index of residential segregation. Logistic regression is employed to determine how being urban or rural, native born or foreign born, literate or illiterate, and younger or older influences the probabilities that individuals would marry across ethnic and religious boundaries. Another important factor considered in Chapter 6 is ethnic status. Canada is distinctive in that it has two founding or charter groups, the English and the French. The former has been culturally dominant through-out Canada with the exception of Quebec, where the French are dominant. Although each of these groups enjoys a charter status, the consequences of marrying into one as opposed to the other is quite different. In addition, the consequences for assimilation differ depending on the ethnic or cultural origin of their mates. This work

considers such consequences for Canada's ethno-religious populations in both the nineteenth and twentieth centuries. The final
chapter summarizes the findings of the study and discusses their
bearing on immigrant assimilation in Canada in 1871 and 1971 in
light of the differing attitudes and policies that prevailed regarding
assimilation.

IMMIGRATION POLICY:
AN EXOGENOUS FACTOR IN INTERMARRIAGE

While the evolution of immigration policy is not the subject of a
specific chapter, the story of ethnic groups and their marital choices
would not be complete without a word about it. Immigration has
been the vehicle which forged the character of the nation, for as
immigration policy changed so did the character of the immigrant
stream. There is no doubt that these kinds of changes are significant
for ethnic groups and their marital choices.

Canadian immigration policy has been subject to frequent but not
radical change. Long-range objectives have not been the order of the
day. In fact, the evolution of Canada's immigration policy from
Confederation to 1967 could be characterized as 'a series of prag-
matic reactions to relatively short-term interests and pressures,
influenced by the emergence of the concept of Canada's "absorptive
capacity" for immigrants at any given time' (Manpower and Immigration 1974b:2) In essence, changes were made in response to the
economic climate of the day, but implicit in most policy changes has
been the notion that Canada should be reserved for the Anglo-
Saxon.

Immigration policy from 1869 to 1945 reflected an interest in land
settlement. Immigration services had even been instituted to meet
that end. Policy favoured British and u.s. immigrants and, to a lesser
extent, Northern and Western Europeans. Other Europeans were
accepted, but only when immigration by the most favoured began
to wane. Visible minorities were unwelcome. The restrictive nature
of early policy was not only reflected in the periodic raising of the
head tax on the Chinese, but also in the Act of 1910. Both the interest
in land settlement and the desire to restrict visible minorities were
underlined in a report from the deputy minister to the Estimates
Committee in 1910. In it, he stated that it was the policy of the
department to do everything it could to keep out the undesirables.
Included among the undesirables were those 'belonging to nationalities unlikely to assimilate and who consequently prevent the building up of a united nation of people of similar customs and ideals' and

'those who from their mode of life and occupations are likely to crowd into urban centers and bring about a state of congestion which might result in unemployment and a lowering of the standard of our national life' (Manpower and Immigration 1974a:10).

Times changed after the Second World War, and national growth and development forged swiftly ahead. The postwar economic boom created labour shortages in Canada, thousands in war ravaged Europe wanted to relocate abroad, and those who came to Canada before the Second World War were anxious to have them. Governments abroad were anxious to alleviate problems of overpopulation and unemployment, while at the same time Canadians saw immigration as a way to develop and populate Canada. In order to address these issues, change and development in Canada's immigration policy and organization were required. Hence, immigration policy evolved more rapidly during this period than it had during the prewar era.

The postwar era (1946-67) has come to be known as the 'second flowering' (Manpower and Immigration 1974a). Immigration both flourished and wilted depending upon the climate of the day. There were peaks and valleys in the size of Canada's immigrant stream, and the emergence of change in its ethnic composition in the direction of increasing ethnic diversity was just beginning. Some concessions were made for Asiatics, such as the 1947 repeal of the Chinese Immigration Act of 1923, and for refugees and displaced persons, there was a new emphasis on humanitarian and social conditions. Those admitted as refugees and displaced persons included Poles, Czechs, Jewish orphans, Estonians, Latvians, Lithuanians, Ukrainians, Romanians, and Finns.

Sponsored immigration became a force to be reckoned with as large numbers of immigrants flocked to Canada. In general, however, policy was aimed at the 'preservation of a system of preferred nationalities' and reflected economic considerations. In this sense, policy during the immediate postwar years and throughout the 1950s resembled that of earlier years. In spite of the emphasis on preferred nationalities and the importance of Britain and the United States as source countries, other European countries, such as Italy, the Netherlands, and Germany, were becoming major contributors of immigrants. Occupationally, immigrants were more diverse during the latter part of the period. While those of the early postwar years were mainly engaged in agricultural work, those of the latter years were overwhelmingly in manufacturing.

A landmark change in the regulations occurred in 1962 in response to growing objections in the late fifties to restrictions on non-white immigration, 'including new pressures from the Commonwealth countries which had recently achieved independence' (Manpower and Immigration 1974a:26). The regulations were amended to state that 'anyone regardless of origin, citizenship, country of residence, or religious belief, who is personally qualified by reason of education, training, skills or other special qualifications' was eligible to apply for permanent residence in Canada (Canada Year Book 1965:205). The implications of this change for the future ethnic composition of Canada were enormous.

Immigrants of the sixties were selected on the basis of education and skills, with preference given to those in the professions and technical and skilled occupations (see Burnet, 1976:201). Because many individuals from the developing countries could not meet these requirements, some control over the character of the immigrant stream was still evident. Nevertheless, Canada made its first move toward non-discrimination in 1962 when it accepted a number of Chinese refugee families from Hong Kong. In 1963 non-white orphans were admitted for adoption, and previous agreements with Ceylon, Pakistan, and India to permit the entry of a limited number of their nationals over and above those admissible under the regulations governing Asiatics were continued.[1]

The introduction of the point system in 1967 resulted in the establishment of nine areas in which immigrants were to be judged in order to establish their potential for successful settlement in Canada. The nine areas included education, skills, personal characteristics, the demand for the individual's occupation in Canada, whether employment had been secured before entry, age, and knowledge of French or English (see Hawkins 1988). The effect of these changes in the regulations not only changed the ethnic character of the immigrant stream in the direction of greater diversity, but also favoured the highly educated, who have been shown to have higher propensities for ethnic intermarriage.[2]

Canada's refugee policy during the latter years of the decade also contributed to increasing ethnic and cultural diversity. In response to various problems throughout the world, the regulations were relaxed in order to accommodate refugees from Czechoslovakia, Tibetans from India, Jews from Iraq, and Asians expelled from Uganda.

Nineteenth- and early twentieth-century policy preserved and increased the numerical dominance the British achieved in the late eighteenth and nineteenth centuries. Changes only occurred as a result of internal pressures, such as labour shortages due to technological change and humanitarian concerns for refugees and persons displaced by war. Nevertheless, the character of the immigrant stream became more ethnically and occupationally diverse as refugees and displaced persons from other European countries and the Third World were admitted to Canada in increasing numbers. The earliest immigrants were mainly agricultural workers, while those who came during the postwar period were engaged in professional, technical, and skilled occupations and tended to settle in Canada's urban areas. Moreover, they were more highly educated than most of the earlier immigrants.

These changes in the character of the immigrant stream as a consequence of policy changes have implications for patterns of ethno-religious intermarriage in Canada. Greater cultural and ethnic diversity, the changes in the educational and occupational characteristics of immigrants, and their increasingly urban location are variables that directly affect immigrant assimilation and ethnic intermarriage in particular.

RESEARCH DESIGN

Ethnicity: A Matter of Definition

Previous research on the significance of ethnic origin for assimilation through marriage has been handicapped to a great extent because of the ambiguity surrounding the definition and meaning of such terms as ethnic identity, ethnic origin, and nationality (Ryder 1955). Additional problems have arisen due to the difficulty of employing such concepts in a manner consistent with their theoretical conceptualization as a multidimensional phenomenon. Gordon's (1964) definition of ethnicity as a multidimensional phenomenon has been accepted for some time (Darroch and Marston 1969; Yinger 1985:154). Furthermore, it has been argued convincingly that it is pointless to treat religion and ethnicity as separate and independent variables when in fact they are intertwined and inseparable (Porter 1965:100; Greeley 1971; Kornacker 1971:152). The tendency to treat ethnicity and religion as separate variables is evident in the analysis of religious trends in general, in the emergence of the triple melting pot theory (Kennedy 1944), and in the writings of those, like Herberg, who have argued that religious identification is replacing ethnic identity (Greeley 1971:82).

The way in which census data have been made available to public users by the government is perhaps another factor of importance. There is no question that the publication of census volumes in the form of preselected cross-tabulations places severe constraints on the level of complexity and amount of detail available. Published standard sets of contingency tables, while necessary for the establishment and maintenance of historical data series and the dissemination of basic census data, have lacked the flexibility required by social scientists for more complex analyses of the relevant sociocultural groups in Canadian society. The production of the 1971 Census Public Use Sample was the first time census data were made available in a form that more adequately served the needs of researchers. Darroch and Ornstein's Historical Mobility Project provides a similar opportunity for analysis of the 1871 Census data. Hence, it is now possible to take into account the basic multidimensional nature of ethno-cultural groups and variations in religious heterogeneity by identifying and disaggregating their ethno-religious components for separate analysis. As far as the sources allow, this research uses a multidimensional definition of ethnicity in the construction of the index of marital assimilation.

Data Sources and Limitations

The data for this analysis come from the 1871 and 1971 federal censuses of Canada. The latter was selected because it was the last census in which a respondent's paternal ancestry was to be reported. This restriction was removed for the 1981 Census and a person was allowed to indicate more than one ethnic origin. Hence, the ethnic data for 1971 are more comparable to 1871 than are the ethnic data for 1981.

The 1871 data are from the census volumes and the Canadian Historical Mobility Project (CHMP) conducted by Darroch and Ornstein. The CHMP is a stratified, random sample of over 60,000 individuals, who were members of approximately 10,000 households, drawn from the original 1871 Census schedules. All of the information from the first schedule was transcribed for all members of the sampled households. Households were randomly selected, but not with equal probability (Darroch and Ornstein 1984). The basic sample was proportional to township populations in that each province was scanned by township and a specified number of sample households were identified in each (Darroch 1986:10). 'The stratified sample overrepresents the urban population in general, those of English origin in Quebec, and of French origin in Ontario and New Brunswick and the German origin group in all areas in which they were at least 10 per cent of the population' (ibid.:10–11).

Weights were utilized to provide unbiased estimates for the national population. The number of cases in the tables are conservative, and estimates for the entire sample are no worse than estimates from a simple random sample of about 3,000 households (ibid.).

The 1971 Census of Canada is the second major data source for this study. The data are derived from the printed products, special tabulations, and the individual and family files of the Public Use Sample Tapes. The data on the Individual Sample Tape refer to individual respondents to the 1971 Census, and the Sample is a representative sample of individual records from the 1971 Census Master File. The sample size is 1 in 100 and self-weighting, that is, each record is assigned a weight of 100. Therefore, to estimate the frequency of any variable for the Canadian population the tabulation variables are to be multiplied by 100. Data from the long-form questionnaire (one-third sample) were used to create the Public Use Sample Tapes (Statistics Canada 1975:1.1.1).[3] Data are also employed from the Family File of the Sample Tapes. It was created by drawing a systematic 1 per cent sample of census families from the 1971 Census Master File. In the analysis, data are presented for the 'head of the family,' that is, the husband in a husband-wife family.

Statistics Canada is required by law to maintain confidentiality of census data. Therefore, the data are presented in a format that prevents the identification of a unique record. Other procedures used to ensure confidentiality include limitations on geographic detail. Geographic areas included in the sample were required to have a minimum population of 250,000. Prince Edward Island, the Yukon, and the Northwest Territories did not meet this minimum and therefore were not included in the 1971 Public Use Sample. The only other procedure involved 'severe regrouping' of certain characteristics which would normally be available at a detailed level (ibid.:1.3.1). Occupation is a case in point, but poses no problem for this analysis since it is sufficient to employ broad categories.

One additional limitation imposed on the analysis is the fact that data for the English, Irish, Scottish, and Other British as individual ethnic groups were not published in 1971.[4] Instead, data were presented for the British origins combined. This aggregation contributes to the underestimation of the amount of ethnic intermarriage in Canada. Hence, data for the British are presented throughout most of the analysis. Given this limitation, the 1971 Census Public Use Sample is still the only large data set detailing the characteristics of the Canadian population available for this research.[5]

Methods

The basic measure of the extent of ethnic intermarriage in a population is the proportion of individuals who have married a person of another ethnic or cultural origin. The intent of most intermarriage studies is to determine the relative cohesiveness of the various ethnic groups that comprise the population and the relative attractiveness of the different ethnic groups for those who decide to marry outside their ethnic origin group (Kalbach 1975, 1983; Carisse 1975; Heer and Hubay 1975; Blau et al. 1982). The relative sizes of the various groups have a direct influence in determining the limits of possible intermarriage that might result from any simple random interaction of individuals in the population (Besanceney 1965; Blau et al. 1982). It is clear, for example, that in any polyethnic society, complete intermarriage is impossible if one of the ethnic groups comprises over 50 per cent of the population. Moreover, research by Blau, Blum, and Schwartz (1982) demonstrates that a group's relative size is inversely related to the proportion of its members who are outmarried.

Most early studies of intermarriage fail to account for the structural factors which influence the magnitude of intermarriage rates (Kennedy 1944, 1952). More recently, however, a measurement has been developed to reflect the 'attractiveness' or 'cohesion' of ethnic or religious groups in intermarriage statistics, while minimizing or controlling for demographic factors such as the relative sizes of the various groups (Glick 1960). Glick calculated the actual proportion of the group that was intermarried and the expected proportion of intermarriage, assuming random pairing, and expressed the former as a ratio of the latter. Milton Yinger (1968) suggested a further refinement, namely, calculating a ratio of the actual to the possible proportion of intermarriages for the group.[6] This index has the advantage of producing a fixed theoretical range from zero to 1, rather than the varying range of Glick's index. Yinger points out, however, that the ratio of actual to possible will be the same as the ratio of actual to expected for any group that is greater than 50 per cent of the total population 'because it introduces a constant ratio factor' (ibid.:98). He also states that the actual to possible index seems mathematically preferable to the actual to expected index. The interpretation of the actual-possible index is relatively simple. An index of zero indicates no ethnic intermarriage, and an index of one is indicative of the maximum possible amount of intermarriage. Because this index reflects the tendency for intermarriage it is referred to as the propensity for ethnic intermarriage.

This research uses rates of ethnic intermarriage as defined by the percentage of husbands who married wives of different ethnic origins, as well as propensities to intermarry, using the index of actual to possible intermarriages. In doing so, it acknowledges that propensities probably do not fully control for group size and sex ratio. The measure is employed, however, as a readily interpreted index that takes into account the size and sex ratio of the population from which mates were drawn by providing a measure of the actual intermarriage compared to the pattern that could have emerged had all those involved in intramarriages also chosen to marry out.

Spearman's rank-order correlation coefficients are reported between the propensities for ethnic intermarriage and various socio-demographic characteristics of groups. The correlation coefficient (Rho) gives a measure of the direction and strength of the relationship and is appropriate where the number of groups compared is small. Its interpretation is similar to Pearson's R, but is usually treated as a rough measure of the degree of association, 'having the same range of possible values as R, but not exactly equivalent to R' (Hagood 1951:676). Rho varies between +1 and -1. The former is indicative of a perfect match of ranks, while -1 indicates that the ranks are exactly opposite. Zero is indicative of no systematic pattern between the ranks.

In addition to the relatively simple method of percentage differences, this analysis employs logistic regression to determine how being urban or rural, literate or illiterate, native born or foreign born, and younger versus older influences the probabilities of being ethno-religiously inter- and intramarried. The logic behind the procedure is to derive an expression for the likelihood of observing the pattern of ethno-religious inmarriage and outmarriage in a given data set (Hanushek and Jackson 1977). This procedure is appropriate because it involves the prediction of a dichotomous dependent variable (ethno-religious endogamy and exogamy) by one or more independent dichotomous variables (urban/rural, literate/illiterate, native born/foreign born, young/old).

It is important to note that the logit model is a special case of the general log-linear model. As indicated by Knoke and Burke (1980:24), 'logit models are categorical variable analogs to ordinary linear regression models for continuous dependent variables'[7] in which 'one variable is taken conceptually as dependent upon variation induced by the others.' Hence, it takes the name logistic regression. In this model, the criterion to be examined is the odds on the expected cell frequencies for the dependent variable or, more precisely, the model to be discussed 'pertains to the log of the odds, called the logit' (ibid.).[8]

In sum, the objective of this work is to develop an understanding of ethnic groups and marital choices in Canada at the time of the 1871 and 1971 censuses. In addition, it considers the application of twentieth-century theories regarding intermarriage and its correlates to the nineteenth century. The research aims to further specify the consequences of marital assimilation in a culturally pluralistic society, especially with respect to the history of the family in Canada. The use of 1871 and 1971 census data provides for a unique comparative historical analysis of patterns of ethno-religious intermarriage.

The Relationship between Intermarriage and Assimilation: Patterns, Correlates, and Determinants

Canada's official emphasis on multiculturalism has tended to divert attention from the normal problems of acculturation and assimilation that most immigrants must resolve in order to establish themselves successfully in this country. Politically and demographically, Canada has been bilingual and bicultural. Whatever their ethnic or cultural origins, immigrants must come to terms with either one or the other of the two major linguistic and cultural groups that dominate Canadian society.

While it is true that Canada has offered refuge to a number of religious minority groups that have been victims of persecution in the past and has allowed them to continue their unique cultural and religious life styles, this has not been the general expectation for most immigrants coming to Canada. Immigrants most similar to either of the two charter groups have always been encouraged to believe that they would experience the least difficulty in achieving acceptable levels of social and economic integration (Manpower and Immigration 1974b). Those who were from ethnic or cultural origins other than northern and western Europe were expected to make whatever adjustments might be required to adapt successfully to the new social and economic conditions.

Studies of immigrants and their descendents have produced a considerable body of evidence showing the nature and extent of the considerable adaptations immigrants have in fact made (Richmond and Kalbach 1980). It is also clear that there are significant variations between ethnic origin groups in their individual members' capacity to become acculturated and economically integrated into Canadian society (Kalbach and Richard 1985a, 1985b).

The purpose of this chapter is to present an overview of the theoretical concerns and research regarding intermarriage and its relationship to assimilation. The concern of this review is to help understand the forces that may have generated ethno-religious intermarriage in the nineteenth and twentieth centuries, to discover some of the characteristics of those who assimilated through marriage, and to set the stage for an analysis of ethno-religious intermarriage in Canada in 1871 and 1971.

ASSIMILATION: THEORETICAL PERSPECTIVES

The convergence hypothesis of classical immigration theory has been central to many studies of assimilation (Lieberson 1963). Its basic premise is that the process of individual adaptation leads to the convergence of the individual and group characteristics with those of the host society over time. The extent of assimilation is normally assessed in terms of the dissimilarity between the distribution of certain characteristics of the immigrant group and the dominant cultural group. The processes of acculturation, that is, cultural or behavioural assimilation and integration that lead to convergence, are numerous and complex, operating within generations as well as across successive generations.

A form of social interaction theory is enlisted in this literature to predict the nature of change between the groups. The expectation is simply that the smaller immigrant groups of subordinate status will experience the greatest change, and in the process can expect to become more like the culturally dominant group over successive generations. Social interaction theory also reminds us that assimilation is a two-way street in that the dominant group will in turn be affected by its minority immigrant groups, but not with the same force (LaPiere and Farnsworth 1942; Gordon 1964:62).[1]

Park and Burgess (1921) formulated one of the earliest definitions of the process of assimilation. They suggested that it entailed the 'fusion' of persons or groups such that they each acquired the 'memories, sentiments, and attitudes' of other individuals or groups, culminating in a 'common cultural life for all' (ibid.:735). Park and Burgess differentiated between assimilation and amalgamation, but included the latter in the definition of the former. Amalgamation was defined as the mixing of 'racial traits through intermarriage,' a process which promoted assimilation (ibid.:737). Park, in reference to immigrant assimilation, suggested that the foreign born could be considered assimilated when they fit into the main stream of the host society 'without encountering prejudice' or discrimination as a result of their ethnic or cultural ancestry (1930:281).

The concept of the melting pot was introduced by Zangwill in 1909. Empirical support for the theory was provided by Kennedy in 1944, followed by Herberg in 1955. Their research findings indicated that ethnic assimilation was occurring within three broad religious groupings, Protestant, Catholic, and Jewish. Social differentiation, then, was sustained by religious category rather than by ethnic origin group. A revisionist view was stimulated by the work of Glazer and Moynihan (1963), who disputed the occurrence of the melting pot and argued that ethnicity persisted in American life. Their study of ethnic groups in New York City revealed that in spite of generational change, distinct ethnic identities were maintained. More recently, Lieberson and Waters offered a reminder that 'theoretically, it is impossible to visualize a full assimilative process if ethnicity is still seriously affecting the choice of mates' (1985:43).

Despite some debate regarding the extent of ethnic assimilation, the dominant theory in the field is still Gordon's (1964)[2] seven-stage model. Focusing on cultural and structural assimilation Gordon argues that cultural or behavioural assimilation usually comes first and that it 'may continue indefinitely' (1964:77). Structural assimilation, which is 'large scale entrance into cliques, clubs, and institutions of the host society on a primary group level' (ibid.:71), either follows or occurs concurrently with acculturation or cultural assimilation. While there is no necessary connection between acculturation and the other assimilative processes, structural assimilation inevitably leads to marital assimilation and is considered to be the 'keystone of the arch of assimilation' (ibid.:81). Furthermore, if large-scale intermarriage takes place the minority group melts, as it were, into the host society, 'identificational assimilation' takes place, and the remaining stages, that is, absence of prejudice, discrimination, value, and power conflict will 'naturally follow' (ibid.). This being the case, with respect to those who intermarry, greater social, political, and economic mobility should be evident and reflected in characteristics that are more like those of the host society than are the characteristics of those who do not intermarry.

In general, three theories of assimilation have been evident. They are referred to as the Anglo-conformity, melting pot, and cultural pluralism/multiculturalism perspectives. Anglo-conformity necessitates the abandonment of the immigrant's cultural heritage in favour of the dominant Anglo-Saxon group's behaviour and values. The melting pot view envisions the formation of a new ethnically blended American. In this case the blurring of ethnic differences is largely accomplished through intermarriage. Cultural pluralism is the most recent of the three and tends to reflect the significance of twentieth-century immigration experience to North America as well as a rekindled international interest in ethnic group persistence and revivalism (Reitz 1980:10). It posits that immigrants take on the behaviour and values of the host society, but at the same time retain certain aspects of their own cultural heritage.

Historically, Anglo-conformity has been the primary model of assimilation for Canada. Hurd, for example, examined intermarriage with the British origin population as a general index of assimilation (1929, 1942, 1964:101). Immigration policy before the Second World War was assimilationist in that it provided for the selection of groups that would most likely fit into Canadian society (Reitz 1980). Large-scale immigration to Canada during the postwar years, however, and the country's unusual position of having two founding charter groups, the British and the French, provided the impetus for the eventual recognition of ethnic diversity in Canada. In 1971 the Canadian government officially announced a policy of multiculturalism within a bilingual framework. Multiculturalism is Canada's version of cultural pluralism. It reflects the idea that 'the survival of ethnic groups as separate groups is socially useful and desirable' and 'as in the melting pot, there is a blending of groups and each affects the other. But unlike the melting pot each group maintains its distinct identity' (ibid.). As Burnet (1987) points out, however, the policy does have defects and ambiguities. The maintenance of many cultures, for example, is not possible or feasible. Immigrants bring their cultural heritage with them to the new land, but many forces impinge upon their lives, making at least some change inevitable. Publicly, government policy is one of multiculturalism, but the ideology expressed by Anglo-conformity still seems to prevail in the minds of policy makers and the Canadian people (Manpower and Immigration 1974a; Secretary of State 1987). The government's policy of multiculturalism, 'which is regarded as an expression of a desire to respect and preserve ethnic heritage for its own sake' (Reitz 1980:44), reflects the greater awareness and concern for ethnic survival that prevailed throughout the world during the 1960s and 1970s. However, the programs announced had as much to do with removing barriers to full paticipation in Canadian society and with inter-cultural activity, and, therefore, assimilation, as they did with the preservation of ethnic heritages.

INTERMARRIAGE AND ASSIMILATION

Certain behaviours are commonly considered indicators of individual assimilation. In a predominantly English-speaking society, for example, an immigrant who is able to speak English is considered more assimilated than one who cannot. Similarly, one is inclined to attribute a relatively higher degree of assimilation to an immigrant who marries a spouse of a different ethnic or cultural origin than to one who remains ethnically connected to his own group through marriage. Intermarriage has been considered an especially important indicator of assimilation since Drachsler's study (1920). Drachsler viewed it as the most severe test of group cohesion (1920:82). Carpenter argued that intermarriage 'provides the most direct and powerful force by which the present and next generations may be welded together into a unified social and cultural amalgam – may in short be truly Americanized' (1927:232). For Bossard the intimate nature of marriage made intermarriage a realistic index of social distance between distinct groups and, therefore, an index of the process of assimilation (1939:792), and for Hurd intermarriage was 'at once an index and a method of assimilation' (1929:23). Nelson called intermarriage the 'final test of assimilation' (1943:585), Jiobu dubbed it 'the litmus test of assimilation' (1988:149), and Hirschman has called it 'the final outcome of assimilation' (1983:408).

Despite this general emphasis, not all scholars agree that intermarriage is the ultimate index of assimilation. Marcson, for example, argues that 'a group may become assimilated without showing a high rate of intermarriage' (1950:78). On the other hand, Price and Zubrzycki (1962) do not agree. They point out that Marcson's theory seems to confuse the notion of integration with assimilation in that a group may be well integrated but not fully assimilated (1962:59). Their argument is consistent with the first stage of Gordon's (1964) model of assimilation. Gordon's assertion that the first stage of assimilation, that is, cultural or behavioural assimilation, could go on forever seems a plausible explanation for the failure of some of the 'older' immigrant populations to exhibit high rates of intermarriage, since intermarriage is not a requisite for cultural assimilation. In addition, older populations that have been reinforced by immigration over the years or have had high levels of fertility would have an easier time finding mates of the same ethnic origin than would those groups where neither is the case.

This research is concerned with the dimension of marital assimilation and, therefore, as generally agreed upon in the literature, uses intermarriage as an indicator of assimilation.

INTERMARRIAGE: THE AMERICAN EXPERIENCE

Sociological research on intermarriage has had three main foci:

causal factors, patterns of incidence and mate selection, and consequences of intermarriage among couples and their children (Barron
1951:249). Much of the research conducted in the early decades of
the twentieth century centred on the physical and psychological
similarities between marriage partners. Burgess and Wallin broke
from this tradition by examining 'the evidence on homogamy for
social characteristics' (1943:109). The degree of homogamy or assortative mating in the Chicago Metropolitan Area for white, middle
class, engaged couples twenty to thirty years of age was found to
vary by groups of items. The rate was highest for items dealing with
religious affiliation, followed by family cultural background. The
lowest rates were found when the psychological aspects of family
interaction were considered (1943:114; 123). In general, Burgess and
Wallin concluded that 'likes married likes' when various social
factors were considered.

Drachsler's study of intermarriage in the United States dealt with
European marriages that occurred in New York City between 1908
and 1912 (1920, 1921).[3] The data revealed that the amount of intermarriage increased from first generation to second generation. The
reason for this difference generally reflected stages of assimilation
(1921:31). Cultural groups in New York City were overwhelmingly
endogamous, but where intermarriage occurred Jews and Blacks
exhibited the lowest rates, while Northern, North-Western and
some Central Europeans had the highest. The Irish and Italians
exhibited rates between the two extremes (1921:35–48). When both
generation and cultural origin were considered the Jewish had the
highest increase in rates from first to second generation and the
Northern, North-Western, and some Central Europeans had the
lowest increase. The cultural groups most often selected as intermarriage partners were the Northern and North-Western Europeans. In Drachsler's view this was due to the higher prestige
enjoyed by Anglo-Saxons as a result of their greater length of
residence and advantaged economic position (1921:57). Drachsler
concluded that the only barrier to intermarriage that seemed to exist
for the Northern, North-Western, and some Central Europeans was
the 'prejudice between Catholic and Protestant.' Colour was a major
obstacle to intermarriage for Blacks, and ethnic religious solidarity
was the major inhibitor of intermarriage for the Jewish (1921:51, 57).

Carpenter (1927) dealt with ethnic intermarriage in the United
States in a 1920 Census monograph. His rationale for doing so was
two-fold. He argued that intermarriage not only controls the cultural
make-up of future generations, 'but it also provides the most direct
and powerful force by which the present and the next generations

may be welded together into a unified social and cultural amalgam
– may, in short, be truly Americanized' (1927:232). Unlike Drachsler,
Carpenter examines data for both urban and rural areas. His findings, based on nationality data, revealed that there were more mixed
marriages for the foreign born in rural areas compared to urban
centres, but the opposite was true for the native born. This was not
surprising given the small size of the foreign-born rural population
relative to the native-born population and the differences in their
sex ratios. Carpenter found that the majority of nationality marriages were endogamous, but when foreign-born men outmarried
they tended to marry native-born American women (1927:239). He
also suggested that when intergenerational marriages occurred it
was probably within the same origin group. Among the origin
groups studied, Carpenter found that the English, Scottish, Welsh,
and Germans married intergenerationally to the greatest extent, but
again, probably to native-born women of the same ethnic origin as
themselves (1927:240). The Jewish and Black groups were found to
intermarry least, and the Irish and Italians again fell in between.
These findings led him to conclude that he and Drachsler were in
agreement at least 'in a general way' (1927:248). Both agree that
opportunity and propinquity exerted strong influences on marriage
patterns for the population and that population size and sex ratio
influenced patterns of intermarriage.

In a 1939 study Bossard also examined intergenerational and
interethnic marriage.[4] Bossard's results were much like those of
Carpenter and Drachsler. He found the tendencies for ethnic and
generational endogamy to be strong. Intermarriage rates were lowest for the Jewish and highest for the English. In addition, he found
generation to be positively and directly related to intermarriage
propensities, that sex ratios among the groups were a basic factor in
rates of intermarriage, and that the intergenerational marriages
tended to occur between individuals of the same nationality or
cultural origin. Overall Bossard found a significant amount of intermarriage by both nativity and birthplace (1939:797).

Interest in the study of intermarriage as a measure of how far the
melting pot of assimilation had progressed continued during the
1940s. Nelson, for example, collected data from rural school children
about their parents from ten nationality groups.[5] Nelson's concern
was that previous studies of intermarriage had all but ignored the
farm population (1943:585). His analysis confirmed small population
size and residential propinquity as facilitators of intermarriage, and
religious affiliation as an inhibitor of intermarriage among ethnic
groups (1943:588–90). Nelson concluded metaphorically that the

Middle West, 'the first great rural melting-pot area of the country,' was not producing an amalgam but rather a 'soup' where the basic ingredients were still distinct, yet with each contributing 'something to the flavour of the whole' (1943:588, 590).

One of the first direct examinations of the melting pot theory was conducted by Ruby Jo Reeves Kennedy (1944, 1952). Her earliest research indicated that rates of ethnic intermarriage in New Haven increased between 1870 and 1940, but, in concert with previous research, she found ethnic endogamy to be prevalent. The highest levels of ethnic exogamy were exhibited by Germans and Scandinavians (1944:332). In an effort to see whether American society was a single melting pot or one with many dimensions, she examined both ethnicity and religious preference. The five largest ethnic groups in New Haven fell neatly into three broad categories of religious affiliation, namely, Protestant, Catholic, and Jewish. Kennedy's findings supported the notion of a triple melting pot in that the increasing ethnic intermarriage observed in New Haven was not 'general and indiscriminate but [was being] channelled by religious barriers' (1944:339). A second report on intermarriage in New Haven updated her earlier work to 1950 and essentially came to the same conclusions (1952:56). Germans and Scandinavians still exhibited the highest rates of outmarriage and Jews the lowest: the theory of the triple melting pot still held. The 1950 data also revealed, however, an increase in exogamy among Protestants and Catholics. This suggests that assimilation was not only occurring along ethnic lines but was beginning to occur along religious lines as well.

Barron (1946) conducted a study of intermarriage in a New England industrial community. Barron's research supported previous findings that the sex ratio and size of a population influenced its propensity for intermarriage. Specifically, he found that 'all other factors being equal, an unbalanced sex ratio induced the numerically predominant sex to intermarry,' whereas a balanced sex ratio tended to favour endogamy (1946:326). Population size was found to vary inversely with the amount of intermarriage, and the number of groups from which marriage partners were selected was found to vary directly with the 'relative size of the group' (ibid.). His research also confirmed the influence of propinquity and generation as factors which favoured exogamy.

An additional factor explored by Barron was the effect of the ethnic make-up of the religious congregation people attended. The findings underline the importance of propinquity for marriage, whether it be inter- or intra-ethnic, since single nationality churches obstructed intermarriage, whereas congregations made up of diverse ethnic or cultural origins favoured ethnic intermarriage (1946:329–30). Most of the research examined thus far indicates that racial intermarriage occurred least frequently, religious intermarriage somewhat more often, and ethnic intermarriage the most. Barron's findings lend further support to those results (1946:332). In the final analysis Barron's research reaffirmed the existence of Kennedy's triple melting pot, at least in the New England community he studied.

Kennedy's thesis attracted the interest of Hollingshead (1950). He too examined marriage license data for New Haven but his were taken from the 1948 Vital Statistics. Those still living in the city in 1949 were interviewed. His purpose was to measure the influence of race, age, religion, education, ethnic origin, and residential class on the selection of marriage partners. No racial intermarriages had occurred in New Haven in 1948, strongly supporting Kennedy's findings. Age was also found to restrict mate selection, especially for women. Next to race, religion was found to be the greatest barrier to intermarriage. In effect, Hollingshead's research confirmed Kennedy's thesis of the triple melting pot. Ethnic intermarriage was taking place, but within the Catholic, Protestant, and Jewish 'pots.' Finally, residential class and education were also determined to have an influence on marriage patterns. While Hollingshead's findings supported the theory of likes attracting likes (he found a highly significant number of cases where individuals married spouses culturally similar to themselves [1950:627]), they also suggested that the triple melting pot was still a reality in New Haven in 1948. He concluded: 'Kennedy's and our data show we are going to have three pots boiling merrily side by side with little fusion between them for an indefinite period' (1950:624).

The idea of the melting pot continued to intrigue researchers during the 1960s. Bugelski, for example, examined the incidence of Polish and Italian intermarriages in Buffalo, New York, between 1930 and 1960. His theory was that if intermarriage increased over the three decades he could 'reasonably conclude that the rate of assimilation is increasing' (1961:149). His findings were consistent with Kennedy's (1944) for Italians and Poles, since their levels of intermarriage increased over the years. Nevertheless, Bugelski was somewhat tentative about concluding that assimilation was increasing in Buffalo, despite conceding that Polish and Italian endogamy seemed to be 'diminishing at a faster and faster rate' (1961:153).[6]

Burma's (1963) study of ethnic intermarriage in Los Angeles, 1948–59, further supported the idea that when intermarriage occurred it tended to be between culturally similar groups. Barron notes that Burma also indicated that the age at first marriage of individuals who intermarried tended to be higher than those who inmarried, unless they were a product of parents who had themselves intermarried (see Barron 1972:128). More generally, Burma found that intermarriage in Los Angeles increased significantly between 1948 and 1959 and, once again, that the size of the groups was inversely related to the amount of interethnic marriage (1963:165). Fitzpatrick 's study of Puerto Rican intermarriage in New York City for 1949 and 1959 also found significant increases in intermarriage from the first to the second generation in both years. Moreover, in comparison to occupational rank,[7] generation was the more important factor explaining outmarriage (1966:405). His findings regarding generational differences support those found by Drachsler's (1920) study of intermarriage in New York City, 1908–12.

Census data provide an opportunity to study ethnic and racial intermarriage nationally. Glick (1970) used the 1960 Census to shed light on the extent of intermarriage for race and national origin groups in the United States and to determine some of the characteristics of those who intermarried. His findings revealed that while rates of intermarriage in general were not very high, there was significant variation among ethnic populations. Nearly 50 per cent of Filipino men, for example, were married to non-Filipina women (1970:297). He also found a considerable amount of ethnic intermarriage among the foreign stock, as well as a significant increase in intermarriage from the first to the second generation (1970:295–6). This was especially true for the Italians and Irish. The pattern of spouses selected seems to support earlier findings. Exogamy was greatest among groups with similar cultural heritages (1970:297). Glick also found that individuals who intermarried tended to differ with respect to educational attainment. Citing the selective process in Black-White intermarriages only, he reported that Blacks who married non-Blacks tended to have higher levels of education than those who chose to marry another Black (1970:293–4).[8]

Most of the research reviewed thus far indicates a direct, positive relationship between generation and the rate of intermarriage. The impression is that generation is by far one of the most important factors related to intermarriage rates, even though Gordon's model views structural assimilation as the key step leading to marital assimilation (1964:71). Schoen and Cohen (1980) noticed that for some groups, such as Mexicans and Puerto Ricans, cultural assimilation seemed to be more closely related to outmarriage than measures of structural assimilation, for example, occupational status. This was also apparent in the work of Fitzpatrick (1966). One exception to this conclusion was the study of intermarriage patterns in 1963 for Mexican Americans in Los Angeles county by Mittlebach and Moore (1968), who argued that occupational status seemed to be the more important factor. Schoen and Cohen reanalysed their data by log-linear methods. Their reanalysis reversed Mittlebach and Moore's findings, leading them to conclude that the importance of generation in explaining outmarriage for Mexican American grooms exceeded the importance of occupational status (1980:365). Schoen and Cohen argued that their findings underline the importance of 'rigour in the analysis of contingency tables' and that 'substantial levels of intermarriage in the United States are more closely related to cultural than to structural assimilation' (1980:365).

As a social indicator, intermarriage has received less attention since the late 1970s except through the work of Blau (1977) and research that emanated from it (Alba and Golden 1986). Blau developed a deductive, macrosociological theory of social structure which 'deals with the effects of social structure on people's associations with other people' (1982:45). Blau, Blum, and Swartz tested two of the theorems with data on intermarriage, namely, that the relative size of a group is inversely related to its proportion marrying exogamously and that a community's level of heterogeneity is directly related to the rate of outmarriage (1982:45). Their major data source was the 1 per cent public use sample from 1970 United States Census, and unpublished data from the 1960 U.S. Census. Their findings corroborated both theorems. In general, it was found that 'the structural constraints of a group's small size counteract[ed] ingroup tendencies and increase[d] intergroup marriages' (Blau et al. 1982:54) and that heterogeneity promoted exogamy (ibid.:56).

More recently, Alba and Golden (1986) examined patterns of ethnic marriage in the United States. Using data from the 1979 Current Population Survey on ethnic ancestry their specific purpose was to examine patterns and strengths of ethnic exogamy. Their findings corroborate the familiar hypothesis that the size of a group is inversely related to its rate of intermarriage. In addition, their research lends further support to previous findings that the groups that intermarry usually select mates belonging to ancestries similar to their own. Although data on religion were not collected by the survey, Alba and Golden looked at those groups which tend to be ethnically connected to the Jewish and Catholic faiths. Their data suggested higher intermarriage tendencies for ethnic groups connected to these religious categories.[9] Alba and Golden conclude that their analysis 'gives something to both sides in the long-standing debate over the place of ethnicity in American society' (1986:218). They suggest that 'those who see an erosion of ethnicity could point' to the historical rise in the rate of intermarriage for all major European cultural groups, while those who see 'ethnicity as retaining its importance can bolster their case with [their] finding that the sharply rising intermarriage rates have not been associated with steep declines in the tendencies for inmarriage' (1986:218). Moreover, they suggest that their findings can 'reconcile to some degree' both positions, since their results also showed that the decline in the salience of ethnicity has not been uniform (1986:219). Specifically, they point out that ethnic boundaries remain salient for those who report a single ancestry as indicated by their high propensity for intraethnic marriage, but that these tendencies apply to smaller and smaller groups because of the increasing number of persons reporting more than one ancestry. Ethnicity is less powerful for these individuals (who are offspring of parents who intermarried), because persons of mixed ethnic origins show much weaker tendencies to choose spouses from the same or similar cultural backgrounds (1986:219).

Research by Lieberson and Waters (1985) using 1980 Public Use Microdata Samples (PUMS) data refutes some findings of Alba and Golden (1986). Lieberson's analysis of the selection of spouses by persons of single and mixed white ancestries revealed that 'ethnic forces are still strong among those of mixed ancestry' in that the children of parents with mixed ancestries 'are still very much affected by their parental ancestry in the choice of mates they make' (1985:49). Moreover, despite evidence of declines in endogamy for the South-Central-Eastern Europeans, many individuals who report two ethnic ancestries also report the same ancestral background for their spouse (1985:50). These findings are in direct contrast to those of Alba and Golden regarding the salience of ethnicity for individuals of mixed ancestry in their choice of marriage mates. Overall, the authors find intermarriage to be 'a strong fact of life for the white ethnic groups in the United States' (1985:45) and conclude that 'the act of intermarriage is certainly an appropriate indicator, ceteris paribus, of assimilation and identification' (1985:50).

One study concerning marital assimilation through ethnic intermarriage that seems to have received little or no attention from sociologists was conducted by the social historian, Richard M. Bernard (1980). Bernard utilized data for ten-year periods from 1850 to 1920 to examine the extent, patterns, and causes of intermarriage in the state of Wisconsin.[10] He was particularly interested in the melting pot concept of assimilation as it pertained to Europeans and their descendants prior to the First World War. Bernard also wanted to test mid-twentieth-century theories about intermarriage on early twentieth-century data. In so doing, he examined both group and individual factors.[11]

The group model appeared to be the most successful for understanding patterns of intermarriage in Wisconsin, especially for Eastern Europeans. Mid-twentieth-century theories, in general, were not found to be helpful in understanding patterns for native-born Americans or Western European immigrants. Large numbers of immigrants in early twentieth-century Wisconsin outmarried. This was especially true for Western Europeans and seemed to be due mainly to their earlier arrival in America, their less urban places of residence, and their larger proportions of second generationists when compared to their Eastern European counterparts. He concluded that acculturation appeared to have encouraged exogamy and, in the process, contributed to the process of assimilation. Bernard argues that his findings provided support for Gordon's (1964) theory of the importance of structural assimilation for large-scale intermarriage, but in his opinion the importance of acculturation for exogamy may have been given less emphasis than it deserved by both Gordon and others. Overall, he argued that the concept of the melting pot regained 'its respectability' when 'surveyed from the vantage point of the marriage altar' (1980:124).

An earlier study of interest included marriage data for the nineteenth and twentieth centuries for the Finnish community in Conneaut, Ohio (Kolehmainen 1936).[12] Kolehmainen found that the marriage data fell into three time periods, 1895–1915, 1916–25, and 1926–35. The earliest period was characterized by marriages between foreign-born Finns. In fact, all but two marriages contracted between 1895 and 1915 were between foreign-born individuals. Because they were young at the time of marriage (20 to 23 years of age for men and younger for females), he concluded that they had only been in America for a short period of time. By 1916 all of the eligible foreign born had married. Thus, new immigrants who chose to marry had to choose a native-born mate. Immigration of Finns began to decline by 1926 and individuals of other ethnic groups began to move into Conneaut. Second generation or native-born Finns now had to select a non-Finn if they were to marry.

Over time, ethnic intermarriage increased from nearly zero in 1895 to a larger proportion of ethnic intermarriages than intramarriages among those of Finnish heritage during the latest period. The apparent causes of the change in marriage patterns included the exposure of the second generation to American customs and the

English language through the education system and length of residence in the country. The opportunity for increasing contact with other ethnic origins and conflict with their foreign-born parents made intermarriage highly probable. The evidence presented is consistent with Hansen's statements (Bender and Kagiwada 1968) concerning the insecurities and anxieties of the second generation regarding their foreign roots and their subsequent desire to leave them behind to become more American.

Pagnini (1988) used the 1910 Public Use Sample (PUS) to examine intergenerational marriages and social distance among immigrants and native-born White Americans at the turn of the century in the United States. Her findings reveal that homogamy was the overwhelming choice for nearly everyone. In addition, the social distance between ethnic groups, an imbalance in the sex ratio, and ethnicity greatly influenced patterns of assortative mating (1988:18–21). On the other hand, length of residence in the U.S. prior to marriage, rural or urban residence, and ability to speak English did not weaken the propensity to intramarry (1988:19–20).

The research examined to this point has dealt primarily with studies of ethnic intermarriage. Interfaith marriages, however, also contribute to the process of assimilation. Only a few studies have been undertaken since data regarding the religious denomination of individuals have not been collected as a part of the United States Federal Census. Analyses of religious intermarriage in the U.S. have had to rely on special studies, church surveys, and limited data gathered by governmental departments or agencies (Monahan, 1971).[13] The studies are of considerable interest, although such data lack national coverage.

As noted, Kennedy (1944, 1952) and Hollingshead (1950) indicated that the rate of religious intermarriage in New Haven was quite low, and as a result advanced the theory that religion was the main barrier to marital assimilation in the United States. Thomas criticized their findings as being too conservative and unrepresentative of other communities in the United States (1951:488). He found variation in rates of religious intermarriage among Catholics in 1949 as a result of such factors as the relative proportion of Catholics in the population, the presence of cohesive ethnic groups in the community and the socioeconomic status of the Catholic population. Socio-economic status, for example, was found to be positively related to intermarriage for Catholics, whereas group size was inversely related to their intermarriage rates. Further, the presence of ethnic sub-groups in communities acted as a barrier to religious intermarriage (1951:489–91). Thomas concluded that his data 'raised

serious doubts concerning the value' of the triple melting pot
hypothesis. Furthermore, he noted that the single melting pot
hypothesis was probably as valid as any theory put forward thus far
(1951:491).

   Locke, Sabagh, and Thomas also found the triple melting pot to be
an inadequate theory of assimilation by testing the relationship
between the size of a religious group and rates of religious intermarriage by region in the u.s. for 1955 (1957:329). Their results indicated
'high negative correlations between the interfaith marriage rates and
the per cent of Catholics for the 48 states' (1957:330).[14] The hypothesis was also tested on data for the ten Canadian provinces. The
results indicated 'a perfect negative relationship between the per
cent Catholics and the interfaith marriage rates' (1957:331). A similar
relationship was found between the rate of intermarriage for Anglicans and their size in the population. In addition, Locke and his
colleagues suggested that other factors, such as the social distance
between groups, level of cohesiveness and homogeneity, and socioeconomic status are also related to intermarriage rates.[15] Like
Thomas's (1951), their research did not support the triple-melting
hypothesis. Instead it suggested that religion did not appear to be
a major impediment to assimilation in the United States.

   In connection with the 1957 Current Population Survey, the u.s.
Census Bureau identified religious affiliation. This survey made it
possible to examine religious intermarriage at the national level for
the first time in the United States (Monahan 1971:86). Paul C. Glick
(1960) found from the data that interreligious marriages occurred
more frequently among Protestants and Catholics than between
Jewish people and Christians (1960:38). An examination of the same
data by Greeley (1970, 1971) supported Glick's findings, but went
one step further by looking at the major denominations within the
Protestant category. Greeley concluded that the rate of interfaith
marriages for Protestant denominations did not vary much. Overall,
including an examination of the National Opinion Research Centre
(NORC) 1968 data, his analysis revealed the persistence of high levels
of religious endogamy in the United States and increasing rates of
ethnic intermarriage. Greeley argues that although individuals were
increasingly willing to cross ethnic lines, it was still very important
to marry a person of one's own religious affiliation, especially for
Jewish and Catholic individuals. Moreover, it was even more important for Jews than for Catholics.

   Abramson (1973) examined intermarriage patterns for 'the traditional ethnicities sharing the Catholic religion' (1973:51).[16] He found
increasing exogamy over generations for Catholic ethnic groups, but

the rates were variable. He concluded that 'the Catholic melting pot [was] not operating uniformly for many different ethnic backgrounds' (1973:56). Mexicans, Puerto Ricans, French Canadians, and Italians were among the most endogamous with respect to marriage. German and Irish Catholics were also found to be largely endogamous, but when they outmarried their mates were generally similar in cultural background to themselves. Irish Catholics, for example, rarely married either Italian or Polish Catholics.

Alba (1976) was also interested in Catholic origin groups and their patterns of ethno-religious intermarriage. He addressed the question of whether social assimilation of these groups was as limited as the research findings of Greeley (1971) and Abramson (1973) indicated. Alba undertook to reanalyse Greeley's and Abramson's data using a revised definition of ethno-religious groups to include those with mixed ancestry. He found social assimilation to be greater than had been indicated for nearly all groups. The differences between Alba's findings and Abramson's were greatest for the old immigrant groups, such as the Irish and Germans. In addition, his analysis revealed that age was inversely related to the amount of intermarriage, while generation was positively associated with intermarriage among Catholic ethnic groups.

A further study by Glenn (1982) utilized NORC data from six national surveys, 1973-78, to examine the trend of interfaith marriages in the United States. His data revealed an overall increase in religious intermarriage for Protestants, Catholics, and Jews. These increases appeared to be due to community size and the differential geographic dispersion of religious populations and ethno-religious groups.

One of the most complete studies of religious intermarriage in the United States was undertaken by Johnson (1980). Johnson's main objective was 'to formulate and apply to American religious data, macro-sociological models of assortative marriage in pluralistic populations' (1980:xxiii). His analysis suggests that population structure, social distance, and the inherent tendencies of religious groups toward endogamy are factors that determine assortative mating. Like most other studies reviewed here, Johnson's interest was in the relationship of assortative marriage to assimilation, but, contrary to other studies, he argued that the popular assumption of the inevitability of the melting pot through intermarriage alone may be erroneous. Johnson's use of macro-sociological models suggests that marital selection is indeed conditioned by population structure, social distance, and norms of endogamy. Johnson's ultimate argument is that endogamous norms arise as responses 'to changes in the group's positions in social space in such a way as to promote group survival' (1980:xxv). In his view this counters the notion that assimilation results in acculturation. As Johnson points out, however, 'the marriage cohort analysis does not fully corroborate the hypothesis of religious adaptation' (1980:xxv). Although it cannot be denied that population structure, social distance, and endogamous norms influence the amount of religious intermarriage in society, previous research suggests that it is essential to consider ethno-religious groups as opposed to religious groups alone.

Generally, research in the United States indicates that racial intermarriage occurs least frequently, religious intermarriage more frequently, and ethnic intermarriage most frequently. Size is inversely related to the amount of intermarriage except in the case of the Jewish; intermarriage tends to increase over generations with the largest increase usually occurring in the third generation. Individuals with high levels of occupational attainment, that is, professional and managerial, are more likely to intermarry than are those who stay in traditional occupations or remain in the same business as their parents. 'Unconventional types' such as actors, musicians, and writers also tend to intermarry more frequently compared to those in the more conventional occupations. Research has also determined that minority group men seem to marry wives belonging to the dominant group. Age also seems to be a factor which influences marriage patterns in that the youngest child of a family outmarries more frequently than either the middle or older child. Moreover, those who intermarry tend to be older at the time of marriage than those who inmarry (see Barron 1972:41–5). The latter finding appears to be the only one contradicted by later research, which indicated that age tends to be inversely related to intermarriage.

Much of the research deals with either ethnic or religious intermarriage. Few studies deal with both the religious and ethnic factors combined, in spite of Gordon's (1964) emphasis on the multidimensional nature of ethnic or cultural origin. It would appear that the triple melting pot theory has been the major catalyst for research on intermarriage in the United States during the twentieth century, especially during the first half of the century. The 1980 Census has focused attention on the increasing component of the population with multiple origins or mixed ancestry as a result of intermarriage and, for the first time, has made it possible for researchers to ask new questions about the meaning of ethnic intermarriage in the United States (see Lieberson and Waters 1985:43–4).

Research findings for the nineteenth century indicate that the majority of individuals married spouses of the same origin as themselves regardless of generation. Size of the group was found to be inversely related to levels of intermarriage.

INTERMARRIAGE: THE CANADIAN EXPERIENCE

Relatively few Canadian social scientists have examined immigrant assimilation in detail. Burton Hurd (1929, 1942, 1964), the foremost scholar of intermarriage in Canada, is one of the few who did. His research centres on the intermarriage between ethnic minorities and the culturally dominant British and French in order to determine the correlates of intermarriage and to assess the extent and speed of assimilation in Canadian society. Hurd's research reflected the widespread concern that prevailed in the early twentieth century regarding immigrant assimilation. Hurd's was the earliest research on intermarriage in Canada and is presented in three census monographs dealing with the ethnic and racial composition of the Canadian population.[17] Because the census did not publish tables cross-classifying husbands and wives by ethnic origin, his data were taken from the vital statistics which provided the ethnicity of parents of the children born in 1921, 1931, and 1941. While there were several 'difficulties' with these data, Hurd argued that they had distinct advantages and constituted a 'highly sensitive index of current changes' in ethnic intermarriage in Canada (1964:97).[18] It should be noted that the interpretation of the data was also limited by the fact that Hurd was unable to differentiate between native and foreign born.

Hurd's analysis provides evidence of increasing intermarriage and significant differences between ethnic groups. He organized his data in terms of linguistic and geographical groupings for each of the decennial censuses, 1921–41. From these data he concluded that intermarriage increased for all groups, but more so between 1931 and 1941, particularly for South, Central, and Eastern Europeans, but overall 'assimilation by intermarriage' had increased most for Northern and Western Europeans (1964:99). The least exogamous of the groupings were the Jewish, followed by the French, British, and Asiatics. Hurd also noted increasing intermarriage with the British over the thirty-year period and a substantial increase with the French between 1931 and 1941. In Hurd's words it appeared 'that very considerable progress ha[d] been made during the past decade (1931 and 1941) in fusing the various ingredients in Canada's "racial melting pot"' (1964:101). Hurd attributed this finding to changing attitudes among second and third-plus generations. Although he realized that little immigration occurred between 1931 and 1941 (see

Figure 2), he failed to recognize the full impact of this fact, namely, that the absence of immigrants, most of whom were already married when they arrived in Canada and therefore likely to have spouses of the same ethnic origin as themselves, would result in a reduction of endogamous marriages (Kalbach 1983:200).

Hurd also examined the correlates of intermarriage. In 1931, for example, he examined the effects that length of residence, surplus of males, size of the group, index of segregation, and rural/urban distribution had on patterns of ethnic exogamy for males and females. By means of a regression analysis Hurd was able to explain about 70 per cent of the variance in the levels of ethnic exogamy for males and just over 71 per cent for females in 1931 (Hurd 1942:651-3). In an effort to explain the residual, Hurd examined various other characteristics of ethnic groups, such as those relating to their social and cultural character, their psychological, occupational, and religious character. His findings indicated that of these factors, religious denomination was 'one of the most important obstacles to intermarriage' for most of the ethnic origin groups (1942:652). Occupation was also found to be a hindrance to intermarriage if the individual was employed in a job that was defined as low status and generally undesirable by native-born Canadians (1942:652).

Similarly, in 1941, the data revealed that length of residence, a large excess of males, and small group size were associated with large proportions of intermarriage for males in 1941. Hurd suggested that the positive association between rural residence and intermarriage revealed for males was questionable, however, in view of the fact that urban residence was found to be associated with intermarriage in 1931. This reversal in the expected relationship for place of residence was thought to reflect the fact that the rural/urban distinction was of less importance as a factor influencing intermarriage compared to the other factors and thus dismissed by Hurd as a 'matter of accident and without any real significance' (1964:104). Rural residence was, however, found to be associated with intermarriage for females. Overall, length of residence in Canada was the most important factor accounting for intermarriage. While similar data on indexes of segregation were unavailable for the 1941 study, Hurd assumed that low levels of segregation, if the data had been available, would have been one of the most significant factors associated with higher levels of intermarriage in 1941, thereby supporting his early findings.

Hurd's analysis of the factors 'making for intermarriage' with the British included an additional independent variable – religion. In 1931 religion was found to be more important in accounting for the variability in the relative levels of intermarriage with the British than length of residence, but by 1941 the converse was found to be true. The nature of the relationships in 1931 and 1941 were the same. That is to say, longer residence resulted in greater amounts of intermarriage with the British. The smaller the group the greater the tendency to marry with the British and the larger the surplus of males the greater the likelihood that men married wives of British origin (1964:108-9).

Hurd was also interested in the degree of intermarriage between the British and the French in view of what it might mean for the fundamental character of Canada. The 1941 analysis revealed that very little intermarriage had occurred between the two groups over the three decades. He cited geographical and cultural reasons for these findings. Included as possible explanations were religious, linguistic, legal, economic, and educational differences between the two populations. Regional concentrations of the British and French populations were also thought to be an important factor, and if they were to continue as Hurd suggested they were destined to do, it would mean that Canada would 'remain fundamentally a two-culture nation' (1942:113).

Hurd suggested that in general some groups were quite resistant to assimilation through intermarriage with the British or the French, but that on the whole assimilation through intermarriage had shown more progress with each succeeding decade. In fact, in his view, this progress was occurring much more rapidly than would have been expected on the basis of his earliest analysis.

Hurd's monographs provide a consistent set of analyses of ethnic intermarriage from 1921 to 1941 and provide the basis for further research. Kalbach (1983) extended Hurd's analysis employing data from special tabulations from the 1961 and 1971 Censuses of Canada. His analysis differed from Hurd's earlier work by focusing on the ethnic intermarriage patterns of those families with native-born heads only. Kalbach's analysis revealed the importance of regional concentrations for patterns of ethnic intermarriage. The French, for example, exhibited their lowest propensities for intermarriage in Quebec and their highest in British Columbia (1983:210-11). Kalbach's data also reveal a similarity in the rank ordering of the ethnic groups for 1961 and 1971 on the basis of their propensity to marry interethnically. More generally, Kalbach's research supports the notion that interethnic marriage is increasing, but at a relatively slow rate, which is consistent with Hurd's findings for the earlier periods.

Kalbach (1975) also examined intermarriage propensities for ethnic groups in Toronto and Montreal in 1971. Propensity ratios were calculated for those families with native-born heads and wives of a different ethnic origin.[19] For both Montreal and Toronto, native-born husbands of Scandinavian and German origin exhibited the highest propensities to intermarry, while the Jewish showed the lowest propensity to intermarry of all groups (1975:71). A comparison of these data with those for Canada as a whole revealed that Scandinavians had the highest propensities overall, followed by Italians, while the lowest propensity was exhibited by the Jewish. Low propensities to intermarry were also shown by native-born heads of British and French origin (1975: Table 5:3).

Jansen (1982) also examined ethnic intermarriage in Canada using data from the censuses of 1951 and 1971. Like Hurd and Kalbach, Jansen found a slight increase in ethnic intermarriage between 1951 and 1971. Moreover, the Jewish were found to exhibit the lowest rates of ethnic exogamy and the Scandinavians the highest in both time periods. This provides support for Kalbach's (1975) findings for the same groups living in Montreal and Toronto. In addition, Jansen found that most groups tended to marry across ethnic lines but not across religious lines. An examination of the correlates of intermarriage revealed that high levels of educational attainment, occupational status, and income status were associated with ethnic exogamy. In addition, exogamous couples tended to be younger than their endogamous counterparts.

An earlier study by Campbell and Neice (1979) concerns social structure and marriage in the province of Nova Scotia. An examination of marriage license data from 1946 to 1966 revealed that the highest rates of exogamy were exhibited by the Irish, followed by the Germans, French, Scottish, English, and Blacks. Campbell and Neice also found that higher status occupations, (e.g., managerial, owner) were positively related to both ethnic and religious intermarriage. In addition, religious homogeneity appeared to reinforce ethnic endogamy.

Other social scientists have also provided information on the marriage patterns of particular ethnic groups. For example, the Jews in Canada were found to have a relatively low outmarriage rate (Kallen 1976, 1977), but an increasing one (Frideres, Goldstein, and Gilbert 1971). Native-born Italians in Montreal were found to be highly exogamous in terms of ethnic origin (Boissevain 1970), and the Ukrainians of Alberta exhibited relatively low rates of intermarriage (Hobart 1975). Carisse (1975) found that considerably higher percentages of English Montrealers married French Montrealers in

1962 compared to 1951, but that the percentages of French outmarriages changed minimally over the same time period.

The United States has been reluctant to collect data on the religious affiliations of its population and, until the 1980 Census, had not collected data on ethnic origin, choosing instead to concentrate on race and birthplace information. On its decennial censuses, however, Canada always asks about religious affiliation and ethnic or cultural ancestry.

Religious intermarriage statistics have been analysed by several social scientists (Heer 1962; Bumpass 1970; Travis 1973; Heer and Hubay 1975) using Canadian data. Heer (1962) presented an analysis of trends in interfaith marriages for Protestants, Catholics, and Jews in Canada from 1922 to 1957.[20] Vital statistics were used in the calculation of the proportion of grooms who married spouses of a different faith than themselves. Kendal's Tau was used to measure the regularity and direction of the trend in Canada and in each province. Heer showed that the proportion of all interfaith marriages increased from 5.8 per cent in 1927[21] to 11.5 per cent in 1957 for Canada as a whole. Increases were noted for each province except Quebec. The same general trend was found for Canada as a whole for each of the three broad religious categories: Protestant, Catholic, and Jewish. The increase in interfaith marriages was greatest for Protestants, less for the Jewish, and least for Catholics. Size was found to be negatively associated with levels of interfaith marriages, but did not appear to be the only factor influencing them.

Bumpass (1970) showed that interfaith marriages continued to increase in Canada between 1957 and 1962. Heer and Hubay (1975) showed that the trend continued until 1972. In addition, size was found to be negatively related to interfaith rates of marriage, which is supportive of the findings of Locke, Sabagh, and Thomas (1957), who found a perfect negative correlation between the percentage of Roman Catholics for provinces and interfaith marriage rates in 1951. They also found a negative correlation, but not a perfect one, between the percentage of Anglicans and rates of religious intermarriage for provinces. Ramu (1976) examined data for interfaith marriages in 1961, 1965, 1966, and 1968. His analysis indicated an increase in exogamy for the Jewish, Catholics, and members of the United Church. The latter consistently exhibited the highest rate of exogamous marriages, the Jewish the lowest, and the Catholics fell somewhere in between (1976:330–1).

In summary, Canadian research revealed a trend toward increasing exogamy for ethnic and religious groups since the early decades of the twentieth century in Canada as a whole as well as for individual provinces. Variations were noted among ethnic origin groups and among religious groups. While the Jewish group consistently exhibited the lowest rate of intermarriage, Germans and Scandinavians tended to exhibit the highest rates of exogamy. Among religious groupings the Jewish generally showed the lowest rates of interfaith marriages, Catholics somewhat higher, and Protestants the highest. It is also apparent that ethnic intermarriage occurs more frequently than religious intermarriage.

Several factors were found to be associated with intermarriage rates in Canada. Hurd (1929, 1942, 1964) and Kalbach (1975), for example, placed emphasis on the intermarriage patterns of native-born family heads because most of the foreign born were married before coming to Canada. This underlines the influence nativity, that is, generation, has on patterns of exogamy in Canada. Size of the group and sex ratio were generally found to be negatively related to rates of exogamy, while educational, occupational status, and income status were positively related to rates of intermarriage, as was urban residence. Other factors, such as regional concentrations and residential segregation, were also shown to have negative effects on patterns of intermarriage.

Hurd has provided the most consistent and the most detailed set of analyses on intermarriage in Canada. The 'progress' of assimilation was his foremost concern. For him intermarriage was 'at once an index and a method of assimilation' (1929:23). In his 1921 Census monograph he concluded that 'certain stocks assimilate fairly rapidly in Canada's melting pot ... while many appear to be practically inassimilable' (1929:25). By the time of his 1941 Census monograph he was able to report definite progress in assimilation, especially with respect to intermarriage with the British and French (1964:18) and for those groups such as the South, Central, and Eastern Europeans, who twenty years earlier, were thought to be largely unassimilable. It would appear from Hurd's work that Canada has a melting pot of her own, different from the triple melting pot envisioned in the United States. In fact, based on his research and that of Heer and Hubay (1962, 1975), Kalbach concluded that the triple melting pot model developed by Kennedy 'has little validity for Canada' (1983:212).

SUMMARY

Previous research underlines the importance and significance of intermarriage for assimilation in Canada and the United States.

Ethnic and religious endogamy have been the overwhelming choices of individuals throughout the twentieth century, even though both have been on the decline. Nevertheless, ethno-religious intermarriage in Canada has been increasing at a relatively slow rate. Twentieth-century findings have indicated that length of residence as measured by generation, as well as age, sex ratio, size of a group, propinquity, educational, occupational, and income status, sex, rural/urban residence, ethnicity, and religion have been important influences on propensities to intermarry.

Ethnic intermarriage has been shown to occur more frequently than religious intermarriage. For broad categories of religion, Jews intermarry least, Catholics somewhat more, and Protestants the most. Furthermore, intermarriage rates showed considerable variation between ethnic groups and a propensity for minority groups to select marriage partners from the numerically dominant group, such as the British, or from groups with cultural and geographic origins similar to their own.

Very little is known about intermarriage in the nineteenth century. Historical data that permit an analysis of patterns and correlates of the phenomenon have not been available until recently. The Canadian Historical Mobility Project (Darroch and Ornstein 1980), which will be used in this study, allows for unique historical analysis. The work on intermarriage in the nineteenth century completed to date has mainly utilized u.s. data. Results indicate that length of residence as measured by generation is positively related to levels of ethnic intermarriage; an imbalance in the sex ratio has also been shown to favour ethnic exogamy. In addition, small size and rural residence have been shown to encourage the crossing of ethnic lines in the search for marriage mates. Each of these factors was found to influence marriage patterns in the twentieth century in much the same way, except for rural/urban place of residence. The latter's influence does not seem to have been consistent (witness Hurd's findings that urban residence was found to be associated with ethnic exogamy for males at the time of the 1931 Census whereas rural residence seemed to be the influential factor in 1941).

It is clear that intermarriage has been accepted as an indicator and a measure of assimilation in previous research. Theoretically the multidimensional nature of ethnicity has been understood (Gordon 1964, Darroch and Marston 1969, Yinger 1985), but methodologically it has not always been possible to apply it to studies of intermarriage.

CHAPTER THREE

Canada's Immigrants: Patterns of Immigration and Ethnic Settlement

In just one hundred years Canada's population increased from 3.7 million to 21.5 million. During this period the annual growth rate has varied between 1 and 3 per cent in response to fluctuations in fertility rates and immigration flows. While Canada is a nation of immigrants and immigration continues to be one of its major sources of growth, the direct contribution of immigration to overall growth has never exceeded that of natural increase (births minus deaths) in the years since Confederation.

The foreign-born population has increased in numbers every decade since 1871, with the exception of the 1930s (Figure 1). However, the foreign born have never comprised more than 22 per cent of the population, which was achieved between 1911 and 1931. The effects of the depression and postwar baby boom combined to reduce the proportion of foreign born to 14.7 per cent in 1951. With the collapse of the baby boom and continuation of relatively high immigration during the 1950s (Figure 2), the proportion of foreign born increased slightly to 15.6. During the 1960s poor economic conditions resulted in lower levels of immigration and the proportion dropped slightly to 15.3 by 1971.

While Canada's immigrants all experienced some of the same difficulties in learning to adapt to their new land, they differed immensely in their social and economic characteristics. Some groups settled in rural areas, while others flocked to the cities and urban centres. Some, like the British, were large enough to dominate the areas they settled; others stayed quite small. There were persisting differences in the status of the groups (Pineo 1987). Occupationally, some groups were predominantly working class, while others were mainly white collar. These geographic, economic, and demographic characteristics – size of the group, sex ratios, and occupational status – were likely to affect patterns and propensities for ethno-religious intermarriage. Overall, the presence of foreign-born populations would reinforce the cultural cohesion of the various ethnic or cultural groups. A better understanding of patterns of ethno-religious intermarriage in Canada, then, begins with a knowledge of the groups themselves.

FIGURE 1

Growth of native- and foreign-born populations, Canada, 1851–1971

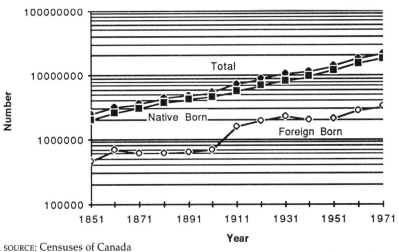

SOURCE: Censuses of Canada

Between 1852 and 1971 over 8 million immigrants arrived in Canada, and while many who came did not stay, this influx has been a vital factor in the growth and development of the country. Of those who came to Canada, some had no intention of staying. Many immigrants and some of the native born were attracted by the opportunities available in the United States. During the nineteenth century, for example, had the loss of population to the United States and the loss of return migrants not occurred, Canada's population size would have been triple what it was in 1867 (Belkin 1966:1). While outmigration to the United States has always varied, Canada lost a quarter of a million people through emigration between 1861 and 1871, and the excess of emigration over immigration was 191,000 (Belkin 1966:2). In fact, during three of the last four decades of the nineteenth century, emigration exceeded immigration by over 100,000 (Kalbach and McVey 1979:47).

Fluctuations in immigration are the consequence of many inter-

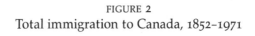

FIGURE 2

Total immigration to Canada, 1852–1971

SOURCE: Manpower and Immigration, Canadian Immigration and Population Study, *Immigration and Population Statistics*, Ottawa: Information Canada 1974, Table 3.1, p. 31

related factors. Economic and political factors in the sending and receiving countries have been among the most important, along with the kinds of assistance offered to immigrants in the form of transportation and free land grants. Active encouragement by governments, the dampening effects of war, economic depression, and famine also played a role in the fluctuations of immigration.

During the 1850s and 1860s immigration to Canada averaged around 19,000 annually, but increased to an average of 33,000 during the 1870s, 85,000 in the 1880s, and 37,000 in the decade of the 1890s. Immigration in the nineteenth century peaked in 1883 when 133,624 immigrants came to Canada (Figure 2). Immigration occurred in large numbers to the United States before it did in Canada, but around the turn of the century Canada's immigration policy became more aggressive. In addition, the government actively encouraged Europeans to come to Canada, while restrictive leagues were being formed in the United States and rigid laws were enacted to help curb the influx from abroad. Moreover, land for settlement was becoming scarce in the United States, while Canada was beginning to expand westward.

The opening of the Canadian West during the first decade of the twentieth century, marked by the creation of the provinces of Alberta and Saskatchewan in 1905, deflected the course of the immigrant stream from the United States to Canada. The lure of the Prairies attracted immigrants in greater numbers than ever before in the country's history. Twentieth-century immigration peaked in 1913 at over 400,000. The First World War, the Great Depression, and the Second World War decreased the flow. Immigration policy gradually became less discriminatory, although it still reflected a preference for people from Great Britain, France, and the United States. However, the flow of immigrants never again reached the pinnacle attained during the era of Sir Clifford Sifton and his program to settle the western frontier.

IMMIGRATION AND ETHNIC SETTLEMENT

At the time of Confederation the population of Canada was just over 3 million. The ethnic or cultural character of Canadian society in 1971 had essentially been established by the time of the 1871 Census (Table 1). This section provides a brief overview of immigration and settlement patterns of the English, Irish, Scottish, French, Germans, Italians, Dutch, Polish, Scandinavians, and Ukrainians. All of these groups, except the Ukrainians, were in Canada in sufficient numbers in 1871 to be reported in the census, and they are the groups being examined in this study of ethno-religious intermarriage.[1]

It is informative to consider immigration, immigrant settlement, and ethnic patterns of geographic concentration, since propinquity influences patterns of intermarriage (Barron 1972; Kolehmainen 1966). This section also presents maps and a discussion of ethnic concentrations in Canada in 1871 and 1971.[2]

The French were the largest single ethnic group in 1871, and constituted about 31 per cent of the population (Table 1). Their proportionate share declined to about 29 per cent by 1971, when they were ranked second in size to the British. The group was almost equal to the English, but was four times the size of the Irish group and about three and one half times the size of the Scottish. The French population has grown steadily over the century. Historically, immigration from France has been insignificant, but growth occurred through natural increase (Kalbach and McVey 1979:28). Immigration continued to be insignificant until after the Second

TABLE 1

Percentage and numerical distribution of selected ethnic populations, Canada, 1871 and 1971

Ethnic groups	1871		1971	
	Number	Per cent	Number	Per cent
British	2,110,502	60.6	9,624,115	44.7
English	706,369	20.3	6,245,975	29.0
Irish	846,414	24.3	1,581,725	7.3
Scottish	549,946	15.8	1,720,390	8.0
Other British	7,773	0.2	76,025	0.4
French	1,082,940	31.1	6,180,120	28.7
German	202,991	5.8	1,317,200	6.1
Italian	1,035	0.03	730,820	3.4
Dutch	29,662	0.9	425,945	2.0
Polish[a]	607	0.02	316,425	1.5
Scandinavian[b]	1,623	0.05	384,790	1.8
Ukrainian	–	–	580,660	2.7
Other[c]	56,401	1.6	2,008,240	9.3
Total	3,485,761	100.1	21,568,310	100.1

SOURCE: Statistics Canada, *1971 Census of Canada*, Special Tabulations; *1871 Census of Canada*, Volume I, Table III:333, Ottawa 1873

NOTES: a Includes Russian in 1871

b Includes Norwegian, Icelandic, Swedish, and Danish

c Includes Austrian, Hungarian, Jewish, Russian, Other European, Asiatic, Native Indian, Other and Unknown in 1971. In 1871, includes African, Greek, Native Indian, Hindoo, Jewish, Spanish, Portuguese, Swiss, Other, and Unknown.

World War. Twentieth-century French immigration reached its peak in 1951 when just over 8,000 immigrants born in France arrived in Canada. The postwar years marked the first considerable increase in French immigration in over a century (Figure 3).

The French settled in Canada as early as the seventeenth century in the area known as Acadia. They took possession, along with the British, of the northern parts of North America. They were the first to establish settlements in what is now Quebec, then New France (Burnet 1987:13-4). The governor of Nova Scotia expelled thousands of Acadians in 1755 shortly before the French era ended (Morton 1983:53; Griffiths 1973:60). Many returned to France; others fled to the eastern United States, especially Louisiana. Later, some returned to Cape Breton, Nova Scotia, and New Brunswick, and because hostilities between the English

FIGURE 3
French immigration to Canada, 1900–66

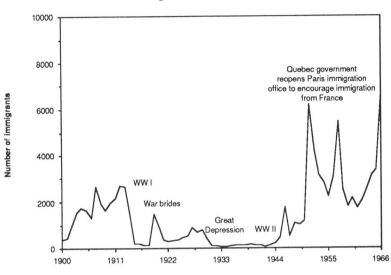

SOURCE: Canada, *Report of the Royal Commission on Bilingualism and Biculturalism*, Book IV, Ottawa: Queen's Printer 1969, pp. 238-45; Dept. of Manpower and Immigration, *1966 Immigration Statistics*, Ottawa: Queen's Printer 1966, Table 7, pp. 14-15

and the French had subsided they were allowed to stay. By 1749 the French were well established in northern Ontario. They were also settled along the St. Lawrence and Ottawa rivers from Ottawa to Cornwall (Secretary of State 1979:86).

The French hoped to build a new Quebec in western Canada based on the foundations laid during the days of the fur trade (Wade 1968:393). In 1818, at Selkirk's request, forty French Canadians arrived from Montreal to join the French Canadians and Métis employees of the fur trade at the Red River settlement, the first colonization of the western interior (Wade 1968:393; Harris and Warkentin 1974:247). Many of the early migrants left the Red River colony by the mid-1820s, but others, such as retired army personnel and traders, settled at Red River, augmenting the population significantly. Among them were French Canadians and Métis (Harris and Warkentin 1974:248). French political influence in Manitoba was lost when the representative of Provencher, Cartier, died in 1873. He was 'the last strong supporter of French interests in the West' (Wade 1968:404). Even though this event signified the death of hope for a new Quebec in the West, the French remained a part of the West. The 1881 Census of Canada reported that 15.1 per cent of Manitoba's population was French in origin (not including Métis). The French populations in British Columbia and the Territories were significantly smaller at 1.9 and 5.1 per cent, respectively (1881 Census of Canada Table III:300–1). The Constitutional Act of 1791 ensured a domain for the French with the creation of Lower Canada and its provisions for the retention of the French language, civil law, and Roman Catholic institutions.

The French, as seen in Figure 4, were significantly overrepresented in Quebec and some sections of New Brunswick, but significantly underrepresented elsewhere in Canada in 1871. A similar pattern is evident in 1971. This compact clustering would appear to reflect a greater level of ethnic-connectedness in terms of language and religion, for example. Moreover, it suggests that low levels of ethno-religious intermarriage would be likely in both time periods.

The Irish were the second largest single ethnic group in Canada in 1871 (Table 1). Crop failures and poor economic conditions were the major causes of Irish immigration to North America. By 1753 Irish colonies existed in Newfoundland and in Halifax, Nova Scotia. More crop failures during the early decades of the nineteenth century again resulted in immigration to Canada. This time large numbers settled in the Lake Erie and Peterborough districts, as well as in the counties of Lanark, Renfrew, and Carleton. Prescott, Toronto, Cobourg, Kingston, Northumberland County, and the Eastern Townships of Lower Canada became home to Irish immigrants. Irish immigration peaked during the 1840s, the decade of famines, poor economic conditions, and typhoid epidemics in their homeland (Mannion 1974:17–18). Large numbers continued to flood into Canada during the 1850s. These three decades of heavy Irish immigration to Canada led to their numerical dominance over the English and Scottish by the time of the 1871 Census.

Irish immigration continued into the twentieth century, but at reduced numbers, never exceeding 17,000 in any year from 1900 to 1966 (Figure 5). Ireland had been drained by the enormous numbers who emigrated during the first half of the nineteenth century. In addition, the Roman Catholic Church and the Sinn Fein party strongly opposed Irish emigration during the early twentieth century.

The Irish were strongest in the rural areas of Upper Canada and the Maritimes with small concentrations in Lower Canada, but were overrepresented to the greatest extent in Ontario and New Brunswick (Figure 6). In Ontario (Upper Canada) the Irish and their children worked as farmers, farm labourers, rural tradesmen, crafts-

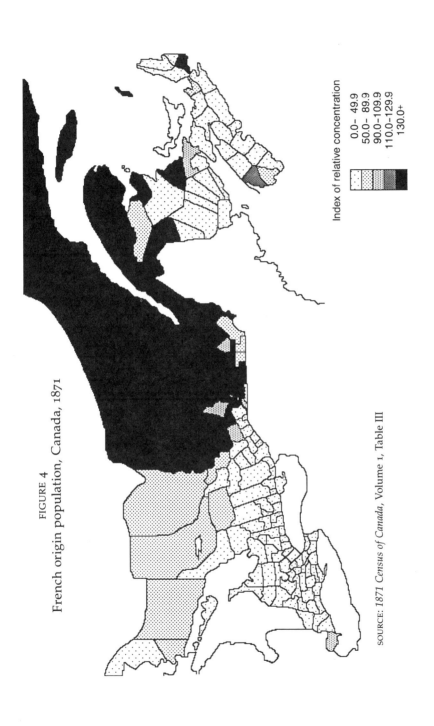

FIGURE 4
French origin population, Canada, 1871

Index of relative concentration

0.0– 49.9
50.0– 89.9
90.0–109.9
110.0–129.9
130.0+

SOURCE: *1871 Census of Canada*, Volume 1, Table III

FIGURE 5
Irish immigration to Canada, 1901–66

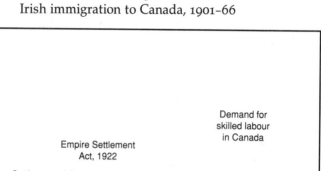

SOURCE: M.C. Urquhart and K.A.H. Buckley, *Historical Statistics of Canada*, Toronto:
Macmillan Canada, Series A316–336, pp. 27–28; Department of Manpower and
Immigration, *Annual Immigration Statistics*, 1961–66, Table 7

men, and, in small towns, as merchants and workers. The Irish of the
nineteenth century were mainly country-dwellers (Akenson 1984:
47), while the Irish of the twentieth century were mainly city-
dwellers who tended to settle in Toronto, Montreal, and Vancouver
(Reynolds 1935:45–6).

Early Irish immigrants included many Protestants, but later Irish
immigrants were predominantly Roman Catholic (Burnet 1972:102–
4). Most eighteenth- and nineteenth-century immigrants were des-
titute peasants, but those of the eighteenth century also included
military personnel and indentured servants.

The English numbered just over 706,000 in 1871 and were the third
largest single group. By the 1921 Census they were larger than the
Scottish and the Irish combined, and remained so at the time of the
1971 Census. To some degree this may have been because of assimilation rather than being strictly a matter of origin. Massive English
immigration to Canada began with the United Empire Loyalists.
There had been some settlement before the American Revolutionary
War, in Nova Scotia (from New England) and in other military
centres. Thousands of 'political refugees' whose loyalties remained

FIGURE 6

Irish origin population, Canada, 1871

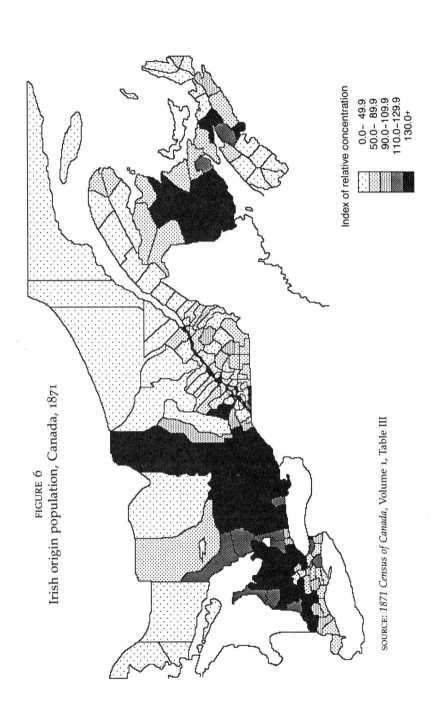

Index of relative concentration

0.0– 49.9
50.0– 89.9
90.0–109.9
110.0–129.9
130.0+

SOURCE: *1871 Census of Canada*, Volume 1, Table III

with the British Crown poured into Nova Scotia and Quebec in 1783 (Secretary of State 1979:72). This influx of United Empire Loyalists created the provinces of Upper and Lower Canada, and New Brunswick. It changed the composition of Canada from predominantly French to predominantly British. They ensured an interest in British culture and formed political institutions modelled after the British system. Immigrants from the United States, many of them English, continued to flood into Canada until the War of 1812. The stream now changed course. After the end of the Napoleonic wars in Europe, it began to flow from Great Britain, especially from England. The English were desperate to escape the depressed economic conditions, high levels of unemployment, and crop failures in their homeland. Thus, by 1819, over half of the British who left for British North America were English agricultural and industrial workers (Secretary of State, 1979:72-3).

Immigrants were almost always adults, but after Confederation English settlement in Canada was significantly influenced by the emigration of children. Between 1867 and 1914 over '60,000 British children, most of whom were English, settled on farms and in towns across the country' (Secretary of State 1979:73). The opening of the Canadian Prairies also attracted a considerable number of English immigrants (Figure 7). Immigration peaked in 1913 when 113,000 English entered Canada from abroad. They came in search of land and freedom from the 'rigidities of English class structure' (Secretary of State 1979:73). The First World War brought immigration virtually to a standstill, and it never again reached such high levels at any time during the twentieth century because economic conditions improved in Great Britain. The Empire Settlement Act of 1922, passed by the British government, was designed to stimulate emigration to Canada through training and financial assistance for immigrants. Under this scheme about 130,000 individuals plus just over 26,000 British soldiers were settled in Canada (Figure 7).

English emigration to Canada did not become significant again until the years following the Second World War. Throughout the next twenty years another large exodus took place, peaking in 1957 at 75,456. Those who came were skilled workers, artisans, technicians, professionals, and English war brides and their children.

According to the 1971 Census, the population of English origin was largest in Ontario, followed by British Columbia, Alberta, and Newfoundland. Both Nova Scotia and Quebec also had sizable English origin populations (Special Tabulations, 1971 Census of Canada). In total, 708,620 English immigrants came to Canada between 1946 and 1973. In addition, England was the leading source

FIGURE 7

English immigration to Canada, 1901–66

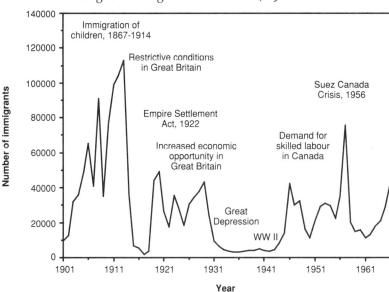

SOURCE: See Figure 5

country for immigrants in 1951 and from 1964 to 1968 and was second in 1960 and 1970 (see yearly Employment and Immigration Statistics).

Although there were a few Scots who fought on the French side in the Seven Years War, emigration of significant numbers of Scots did not begin until 1760 when New France came under British rule. Between 1750 and the end of the century a continuous stream, which gathered momentum from the latter years of the 1700s until the end of the nineteenth century, made its way to Canada. Spurred on by unemployment, the dislocation of many farmers from their land, the successive years of potato famine (the worst being in 1845), the decline of the fishing industry, and general economic depression, 'the stream became a torrent' for most of the nineteenth century (Secretary of State 1979:191). Cape Breton, Pictou County, and other parts of Nova Scotia became home to many Scots in the 1790s. They quickly formed Scottish enclaves whose members spoke only Gaelic. Scots were also among the United Empire Loyalists who came to Nova Scotia and New Brunswick in the late 1780s.

The Scots came to Canada in three waves, each larger than its predecessor. The first wave occurred between 1763 and 1815, followed by the second, which began in 1815 and lasted until 1870, which brought 170,000 Scots to Canada. The sheer number of individuals established the Scots 'as one of the major ethnic components of the Canadian population' (Bumstead 1982:10, 13). During the second wave, Scottish immigrants tended to cluster where their counterparts had settled during the first wave. This included the north coast of Nova Scotia and Cape Breton, Prince Edward Island, and the eastern districts of Upper Canada and Lower Canada, where they concentrated in the Eastern Townships (Bumstead 1982:10–1). In Upper Canada, the favoured destinations were Lanark County, Renfrew County, and the northern shores of Lake Erie. Other centres of Scottish settlement were Guelph, Galt, Goderich, and the counties of Huron and Bruce (Secretary of State 1979:192–3). At the time of the 1871 Census, the Scots were the fourth largest ethnic group in the four original provinces.

The Scots continued to flood into Canada in great numbers between 1870 and 1930. This third wave was the largest and 517,000 Scots came to Canada during this period. Their pattern of immigration was much like that of the English and the Irish (Bumstead 1982:10). The peak years were the early decades. Nearly 125,000 Scots came between 1910 and 1913 at the height of western settlement (Figure 8). During the war Scottish immigration declined, but

FIGURE 8
Scottish immigration to Canada, 1901–66

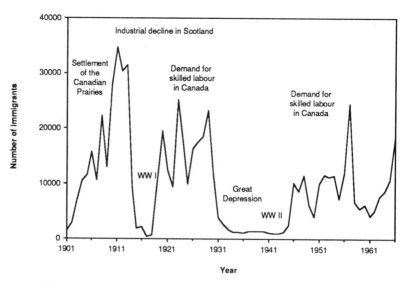

SOURCE: See Figure 5

increased again during the twenties when the economic and political climate in the British Isles was poor. It slowed to a trickle during the thirties and early forties and flourished once again in the fifties, peaking in 1957 when 24,533 Scots arrived in Canada (Urquhart and Buckley 1965:27-8, Figure 8). The Scottish comprised 8 per cent of the Canadian population by the time of the 1971 Census, a decline of 7.8 percentage points from 15.8 per cent in 1871.

The Scots came in great numbers to all of the provinces except for Newfoundland and Quebec. Most settled in Ontario and the West, except for those attracted by the coal mines of Nova Scotia. Some who settled in the West were in agricultural occupations, but most went to the urban areas engaging in business, industry, and education (Bumstead 1982).

As expected, the British ethnic groups tended to be more heavily concentrated in Ontario and the Atlantic regions in 1871 (Figures 6, 9, and 10). Due to the numerical dominance of the Irish there was some overlap with both the English and the Scottish, while the English and the Scottish did not tend to overlap to the same extent. These patterns of relative concentration suggest that if ethno-religious intermarriage were to occur these British ethnic groups would likely tend to favour each other to the greatest extent. It is also likely that English spouses would be favoured by the Irish and Scottish because of their cultural and economic dominance, as well as their cultural similarity. Similar conclusions regarding marital choices could still be made in 1971. The British still tended to be overrepresented in Ontario and the Atlantic provinces in 1971. They were also overrepresented in British Columbia and Newfoundland. It is important to note that by 1971 the English were numerically dominant as well as culturally and economically dominant.

The Germans have ranked third behind the British and French in every census since Confederation. German immigration to Canada occurred in three waves, 1749-1870, 1870-1914, and 1951-60 (McLaughlin 1985), with each being larger than the previous one. The history of German settlement began with the first wave, when 2,000 of them (recruited by Britain) were settled in Halifax and Lunenburg (Lehmann 1986:10). Germans were among the Loyalists who came during the early nineteenth century. Many were Mennonites seeking freedom from military service and the right to practise their religion. They settled in present-day Lincoln County in Ontario in the Niagara region. According to Lehmann the movement of Mennonites from Pennsylvania into Upper Canada continued until the second decade of the nineteenth century. Over 2,000 Mennonites came in this period, settling in what is now Kitchener-

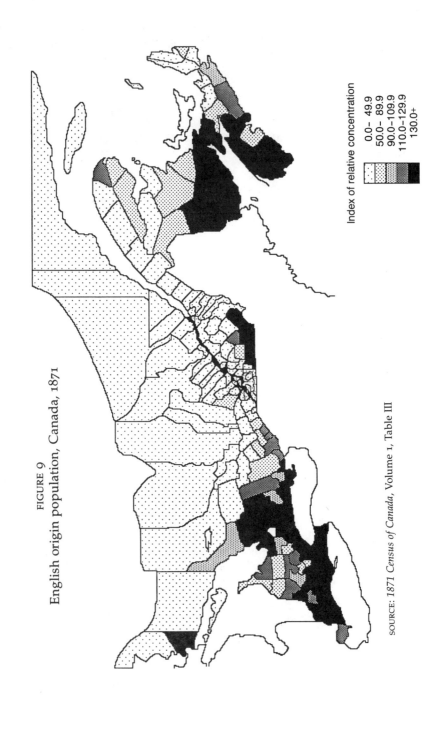

FIGURE 9
English origin population, Canada, 1871

Index of relative concentration

0.0– 49.9
50.0– 89.9
90.0–109.9
110.0–129.9
130.0+

SOURCE: 1871 *Census of Canada*, Volume 1, Table III

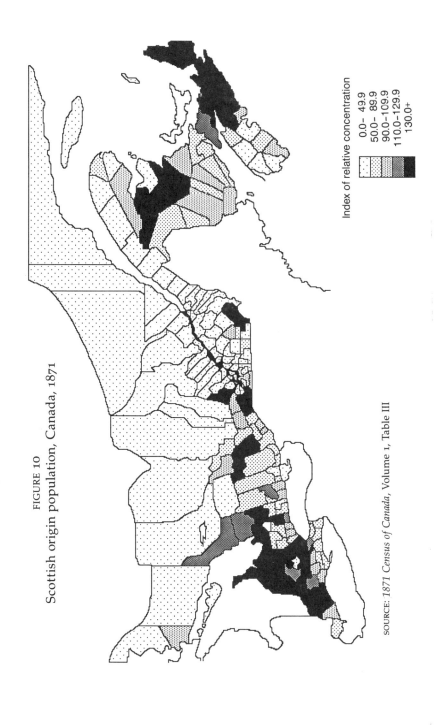

FIGURE 10

Scottish origin population, Canada, 1871

Index of relative concentration

0.0- 49.9
50.0- 89.9
90.0-109.9
110.0-129.9
130.0+

SOURCE: *1871 Census of Canada*, Volume I, Table III

Waterloo, Markham, Whitchurch Township (York County), and Ontario County (1986:14). Lehmann notes that 'hundreds, even thousands of German Americans seem to have come to southern Ontario in the early years of its colonization, yet they were scattered in groups of varied size' (1986:16).

Up to this point most German immigrants coming to Canada were from Pennsylvania and New York. By the 1830s the number of German Americans declined. They were replaced by immigrants from Germany driven from their homeland by the potato blight, crop failures, and generally poor economic conditions. The flow from Germany continued from 1830 to 1870. Most of those who came from Germany were farmers or craftsmen, and almost all settled in southwestern Ontario. A few craftsmen went to Montreal and a few farmers were given land in the Ottawa district (Lehmann 1986:18). Upper Canada's apparent prosperity proved tempting to nearly 50,000 immigrants of German ethnic origin between 1830 and 1871 (Gibbon 1938:177–8). By the 1871 Census, 158,000 Germans had settled in Ontario, and the number of Germans in Canada as a whole numbered 202,991, or 5.8 per cent of the population.

Figure 11 presents the significant highs and lows of German immigration to Canada from 1900 to 1966. It can be seen that the second wave coincided with the opening of the Canadian West, and that is where most German immigrants went. The majority who came during this period were pioneers and farmers who settled in the rural areas, while others went to the urban areas of Winnipeg, Calgary, and Regina. British Columbia had a German population as early as 1857. After 1870, farmers came to settle the province's interior, while the shopkeepers, professionals, businessmen, and artisans went to such urban centres as Vancouver and Victoria. Ontario, unlike British Columbia, did not attract many German immigrants during the early twentieth century (McLaughlin 1985). Nearly 152,000 Germans resided in the West by the time of the 1911 Census. Of all the German immigrants only the Mennonites and Catholics established bloc settlements in Western Canada; the others were scattered 'over the entire west' (Lehmann 1986:132).

Prior to 1914 Germans were among the favoured immigrants. The First World War changed that view, and German immigration virtually ceased. Germans who were already in Canada were unwilling to admit to being German in origin. The repeal of war-time restrictions made possible an unprecedented flow of German immigrants to Canada between 1928 and 1930 (see Figure 11).

The years from 1951 to 1967 saw an additional influx of German immigrants, most of whom were economic immigrants. Their char-

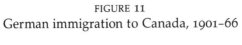

FIGURE 11

German immigration to Canada, 1901–66

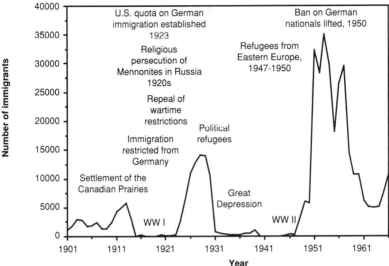

SOURCE: See Figure 5

acteristics differed from earlier German immigrants. Most were married, widowed, or divorced and 40 per cent were twenty-five to thirty-four years of age. They were well educated and by the 1960s had the highest proportion of postwar European immigrants speaking English (McLaughlin 1985:17). Their primary destinations were Toronto, Montreal, and Vancouver. The flow of German immigrants began to decline by 1970, but, by the 1971 Census, those of German origin in Canada numbered just over one million or 6.1 per cent (Table 1). In 1871 German areas of relatively high concentration show some overlap with the English areas, particularly in Ontario (Figure 12). One hundred years later this was still true for the most part, but in the Prairie provinces they overlapped with the Poles, Ukrainians, Dutch, and Scandinavians.

Even though Italian immigration to Canada was a twentieth-century phenomenon, it began in the later decades of the nineteenth century, when significant numbers of peasants from the south emigrated to South America, the United States, and Canada in order to improve their lot. By 1871, 1,035 Italians lived in Canada. The movement of Italians to Canada in the early decades of the twentieth century was a response to the need for unskilled labour (Figure 13). By 1901 there were 10,000 Italians in Canada. Seven years later,

FIGURE 12

German origin population, Canada, 1871

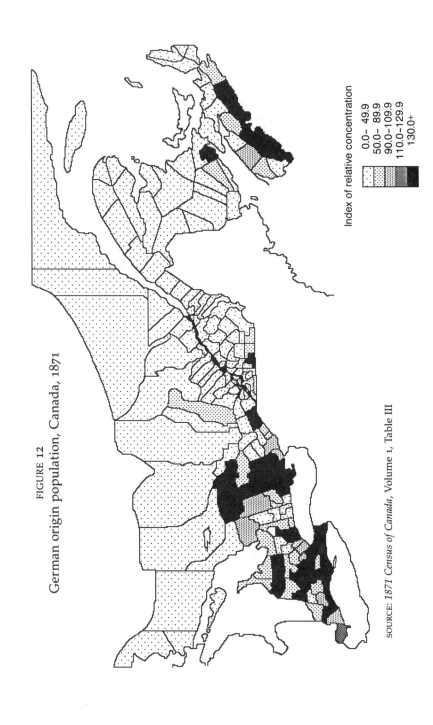

Index of relative concentration

0.0– 49.9
50.0– 89.9
90.0–109.9
110.0–129.9
130.0+

SOURCE: *1871 Census of Canada*, Volume 1, Table III

FIGURE 13

Italian immigration to Canada, 1900–66

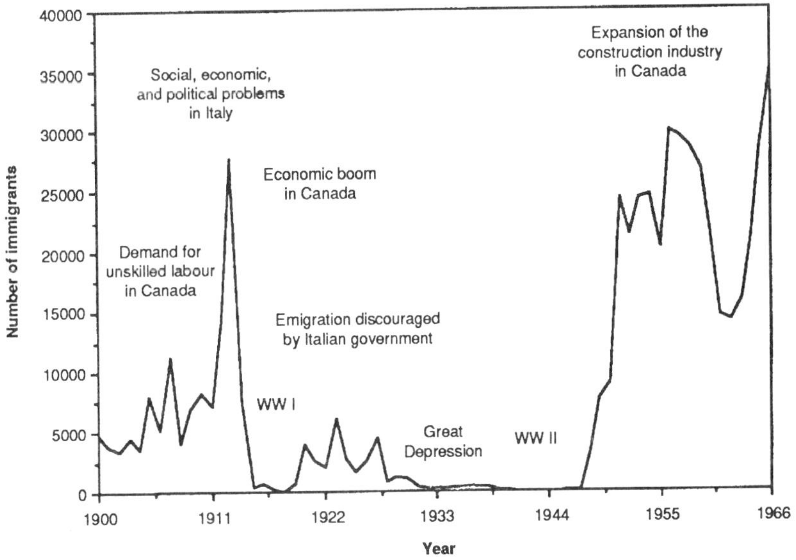

SOURCE: See Figure 5

50,000 resided here (Woodsworth 1909:131). Many of the immigrants were labourers and many had been fruit farmers in their homeland, but few went into agricultural occupations in Canada. Instead they worked in the mines and in the construction industry (Avery 1979). While the majority of Italian immigrants of the early decades were relatively uneducated and unskilled, some were bankers and tailors. They were so overrepresented in the construction industry, however, that Woodsworth (1909) dubbed them 'the pick and shovel brigade.' The first wave (1900–14) of Italian immigrants totalled nearly 120,000, and was concentrated in Montreal. Immigration was slowed to a trickle during the Great Wars, but assumed major proportions during the postwar period. More than 400,000 Italians arrived in Canada between 1946 and 1966 in response to the country's need for unskilled labour. Post Second World War Italians settled mainly in Toronto, making it the largest 'Italian' city in Canada by 1971. Italian industrial workers also settled in such places as Hamilton, Sudbury, the Lakehead, and Sault Ste. Marie. According to the 1971 Census of Canada, Ontario was home to over 60 per cent of the Italian population in Canada. Quebec and British Columbia had the next largest Italian populations, and substantial numbers also resided in Alberta and Manitoba. They were indeed overrepresented, as seen in Figure 14, in Vancouver, Toronto, Montreal, and the mining areas of Alberta and Ontario.

The social, economic, and political problems that encouraged British immigrants to flee their homeland in droves did not plague the Dutch until the mid-nineteenth century. Immigration to the United States occurred first and it was not until land became scarce in the u.s. that the Dutch came to Canada in large numbers. The first Dutch settlers came with the United Empire Loyalists, settling mainly in Upper Canada and the Maritimes (Palmer 1972:14). Even though Dutch migration to Canada remained small until the opening of the West, there were 29,662 living in Canada in 1871, according to the census.

The overseas Dutch and the American Dutch were attracted by the availability of free or cheap land in the West. In 1892 a group of single men arrived in Winnipeg to work on the railway and farms. During the same year a Dutch colony was begun at Yorkton, Saskatchewan. The settlers found the rigours of prairie life too difficult to endure, so they left for Winnipeg, where they succeeded in establishing a Dutch community (Palmer 1972:14). Dutch immigration only numbered twenty-five in 1900 but steadily increased until 1913, when it peaked at 1,700 (Figure 15). As land became scarce in Canada's West, the mixed farming areas of southwestern Ontario became the destination for most Dutch immigrants. During the years from 1924 to 1930 over 10,000 arrived in Canada. Postwar immigration was substantial until 1960. It began with 2,146 immigrants in 1946 and rose to its pinnacle in 1952 when just over 21,000 arrived in Canada. A slightly smaller peak of 20,000 occurred one year later (Figure 15).

Dutch immigrants were primarily involved in agricultural occupations. By 1953 significant numbers engaged in managerial, professional, and technical occupations, who were seeking a better economic future for their families, found their way to Canada's urban centres, along with many Dutch war brides. The major centres for postwar immigration settlement were located in the provinces of Ontario, Alberta, and British Columbia (Gibbon 1938:203; Palmer 1972:19). The Dutch increased their proportionate share of the Canadian population from 0.9 per cent in 1871 to 2 per cent in 1971.

In 1871 the Dutch were most heavily concentrated in districts where the English showed relatively high indexes of concentration (Figure 16). The immigration and settlement patterns of the Dutch during the first seventy years of the twentieth century are reflected in their patterns of relative concentration (Figure 17). They were

FIGURE 14
Italian origin population,
Canada, 1971

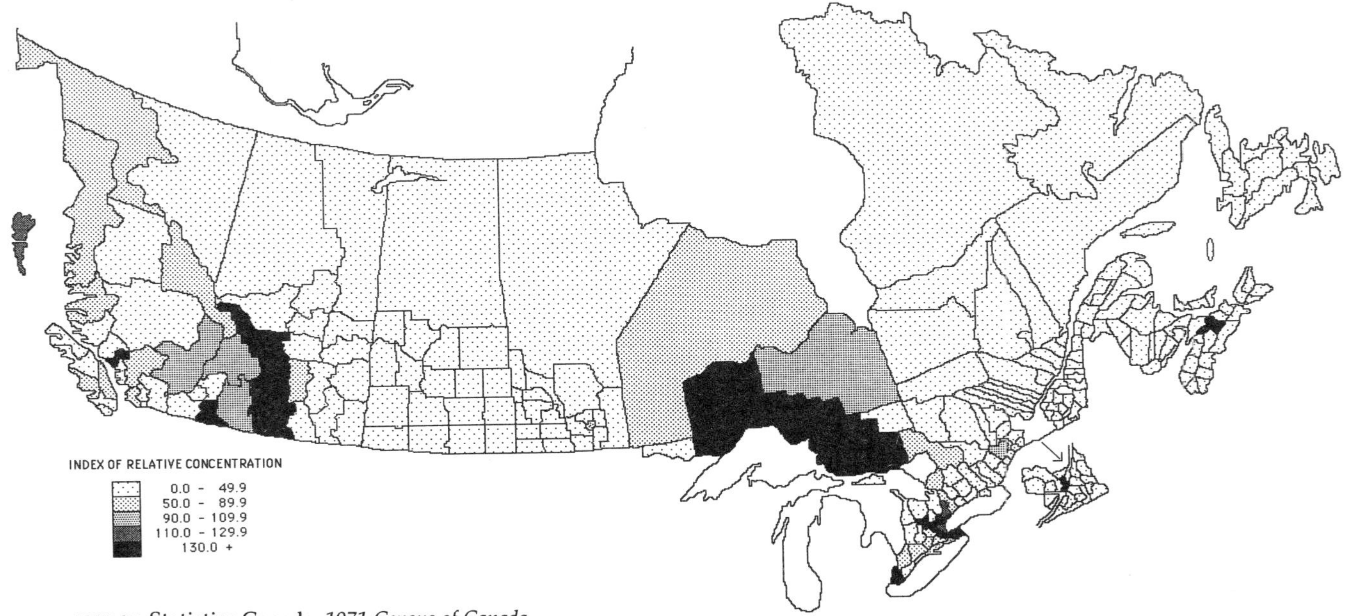

INDEX OF RELATIVE CONCENTRATION

0.0 - 49.9
50.0 - 89.9
90.0 - 109.9
110.0 - 129.9
130.0 +

SOURCE: Statistics Canada, *1971 Census of Canada*

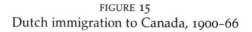

FIGURE 15
Dutch immigration to Canada, 1900–66

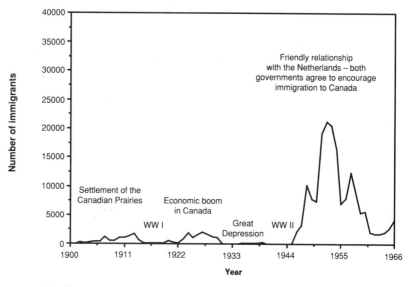

SOURCE: See Figure 5

significantly overrepresented in British Columbia and Alberta, and in parts of Saskatchewan, Manitoba, and Ontario. They were underrepresented in Eastern Canada, with the exception of Nova Scotia.

Aside from a few individuals and a small group of Kashoubs who came to the Renfrew area around 1860 (Makowski 1967:53), the Poles came to Canada in three distinct waves. The first wave began in the late nineteenth century and ended prior to 1914 (Figure 18). The immigrants were attracted by employment opportunities with the railways or land on the Prairies (Avery and Fedorowicz 1982:7). The Poles responded to Sifton's request for European agricultural workers. They settled in large blocs east of Winnipeg where they 'transformed the land into a prosperous mixed farming district,' then the immigrant stream moved on through Manitoba into Saskatchewan and Alberta (Gibbon 1938:271). In 1907 over 15,000 Poles came in search of land, employment, and a better life. This first period of immigration was characterized by two different streams. One consisted of families and individuals who were searching for land or employment, while the other was made up of temporary sojourners who came 'only to find work, save, and return,' and this group made up the majority (Radecki and Heydenkorn 1976:28).

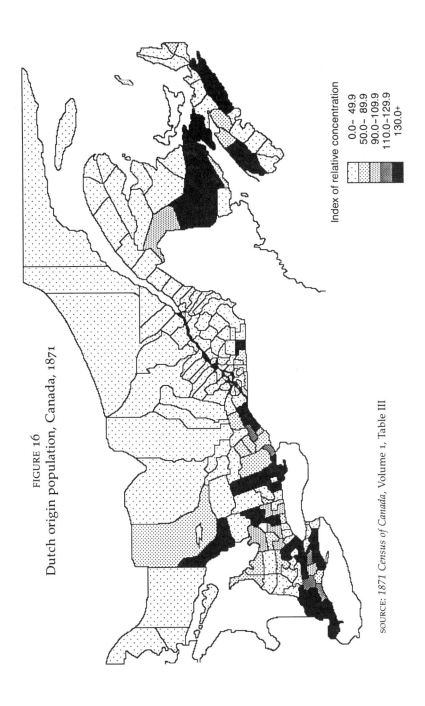

FIGURE 16
Dutch origin population, Canada, 1871

Index of relative concentration

0.0– 49.9
50.0– 89.9
90.0–109.9
110.0–129.9
130.0+

SOURCE: *1871 Census of Canada*, Volume 1, Table III

FIGURE 17
Dutch origin population,
Canada, 1971

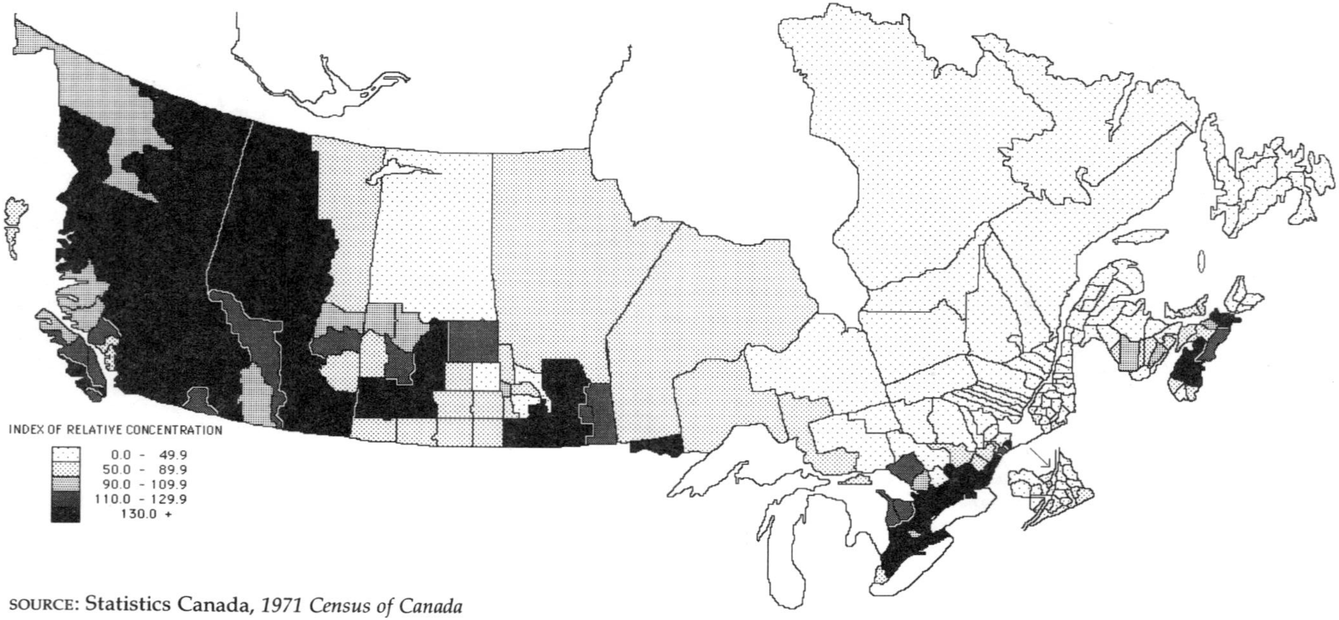

INDEX OF RELATIVE CONCENTRATION

0.0 - 49.9
50.0 - 89.9
90.0 - 109.9
110.0 - 129.9
130.0 +

SOURCE: Statistics Canada, 1971 *Census of Canada*

The second wave of Polish immigrants to Canada began in 1919 and ended in 1930 (Figure 18). Following the war, Poland experienced tremendous political, social, and economic upheaval. The Polish government sent a delegation to investigate Canadian conditions, because immigration to the United States was being curtailed through quotas. Canada's doors were still open and opportunities awaited. Poles were encouraged to emigrate to Canada so they could take advantage of agricultural and industrial opportunities. Nearly 52,000 Poles responded to that encouragement between 1919 and 1931 (Figure 18). The vast majority were still concentrated in agriculture and semi-skilled labour, but many were artisans and shopkeepers. Some still came as sojourners, but they were fewer (Radecki and Heydenkorn 1976:31).

FIGURE 18
Polish immigration to Canada, 1900–66

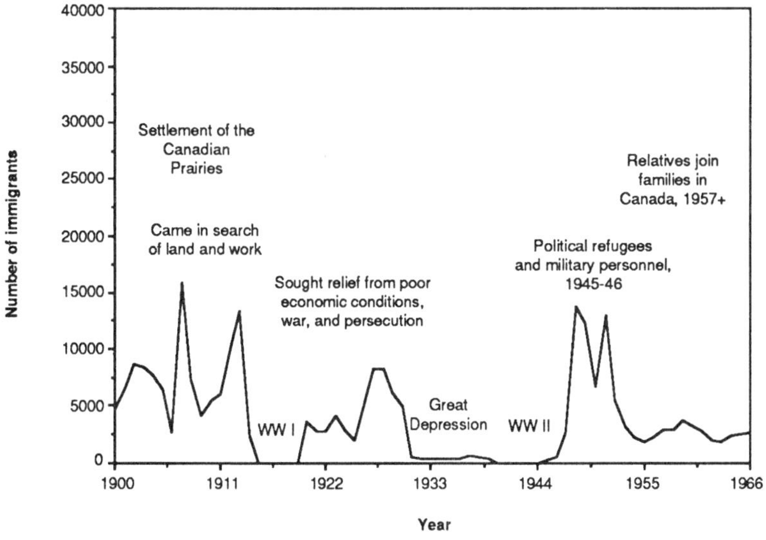

SOURCE: See Figure 5

During the Second World War, direct immigration from Poland ceased and did not resume again until 1957 (Radecki and Heydenkorn 1976:32). While most Poles stayed in Poland to fight in the underground, others escaped so they could serve with or help the allies. Between 1941 and 1942 nearly 1,000 highly skilled technicians and professionals came to assist in Canada's war effort. They were not regarded as immigrants at the time, but as temporary workers (Radecki and Heydenkorn 1976:32).

The third wave began in 1945 (Figure 18). It began slowly, peaking between 1948 and 1951, when nearly 46,000 Poles entered Canada. The immigrants of this wave differed from their earlier counterparts. Many were brought in through the efforts of the Canadian and British governments and 'Polish government-in-exile.' Those who came during the peak years were Polish refugees (including Polish Jews) admitted under the refugee program and some 4,500 war veterans, who came under a special plan. The large influx was facilitated by a healthy economic climate in Canada, an improvement in attitudes toward Jews, and a loosening of immigration policy in the fifties and sixties.

Unlike those who came to Canada before them, Poles of the third wave era were motivated by political concerns. They were highly skilled, well educated, aged thirty to thirty-five on the average, and men outnumbered women three to one. Many were ex-soldiers. Having undergone the ravages and mistreatments caused by war, most of the Poles who came to Canada during the postwar years entered from countries other than Poland, where they had settled before relocating to Canada for economic reasons. Their major motivation was to escape oppression and to seek political freedom (Radecki and Heydenkorn 1976:33-4; Avery et al. 1982: 13-4).

In 1957 immigration directly from Poland resumed, but on a smaller scale than in the previous postwar years. A few years of liberalized government in Poland resulted in the reunification of families and the arrival of many brides-to-be, who had been sought out on visits to the homeland or who had been arranged for through other means. Refugees and war veterans also continued to trickle in (Radecki and Heydenkorn 1976: 34-5).

The 1871 Census reveals that only 607 Poles were resident in Canada at that time, and this number included Russians. By the 1971 Census the Polish population numbered just over 316,000. According to the censuses of Canada over half of the Poles lived in Ontario in 1871, and the vast majority of the Polish population still resided in Ontario, a century later. As shown in Figure 19, by 1971 they were significantly overrepresented in Ontario, Alberta, and the southern districts of Saskatchewan and Manitoba. They were significantly underrepresented in Quebec and eastern Canada. Their concentrations in bloc settlements on the Prairies overlapped with the Germans, Ukrainians, and Scandinavians. There was also some overlap with the British areas of concentration. While bloc settlement may have facilitated marriage within their own ethnic group, when Poles

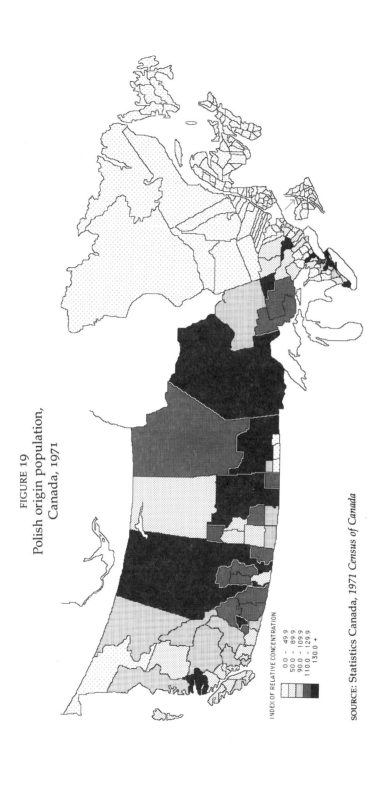

FIGURE 19
Polish origin population,
Canada, 1971

INDEX OF RELATIVE CONCENTRATION

0.0 - 49.9
50.0 - 89.9
90.0 - 109.9
110.0 - 129.9
130.0 +

SOURCE: Statistics Canada, *1971 Census of Canada*

did choose spouses from a different ethnic origin, it was likely to be British, German, Ukrainian, or Scandinavian.

The 1871 and 1971 censuses of Canada include the Danes, Icelanders, Norwegians, and Swedes in the Scandinavian ethnic origin group. Woodsworth (1909) is one of the few who wrote about Scandinavians as a group. He found that they assimilated easily through intermarriage, learning to speak English and mingling well 'with the families of Canadian farmers' (1909:91). As a result, he noted that Scandinavians were found everywhere in the West and, unlike other European immigrants, did not tend to settle in isolated colonies.

Scandinavians began coming to Canada in the nineteenth century. Danish immigrants were among the earliest settlers of the group. Danish farmers, for example, created their first settlement in 1835 near present-day Port Arthur, Ontario. Swedish and Icelandic immigration to Canada began in the 1870s, and Norwegian immigration began in earnest two decades later. The vast majority of Scandinavians who came in the nineteenth and early twentieth centuries went to the Prairies, motivated by the scarcity of land in the United States and the chance for free land in Canada. Most of these early immigrants were farmers, but many were employed by the Canadian Pacific Railway as construction workers. Others worked as lumberjacks and miners.

Not all the Scandinavians were lured by the land of the Prairies. In the 1870s Danes settled in New Brunswick and, by 1893, had also settled in London and near Thunder Bay in Ontario. Icelanders also settled in the Maritimes near Halifax and Lockport in 1874 (see Woodsworth 1909:93 and *Ontario Ethnocultural Profiles* of Icelanders 1979). Woodsworth indicates that of the four individual ethnic groups included under the term 'Scandinavians,' the Icelanders were the most successful. In fact they were so successful that in 1876 the Canadian government sought them out. As a result, 1,600 Icelanders were enticed to settle in Canada's West.

By the turn of the century, Scandinavians were scattered from Fort William to the Coast. Winnipeg was the largest settlement in the province of Manitoba; Saskatchewan settlers tended to settle along the Canadian Northern railway line. Alberta had the largest number of Scandinavians of all the provinces just after the turn of the century, most of whom were extremely successful farmers. Those who lived in British Columbia farmed the valleys. Others lived in Vancouver and along the banks of the Fraser River. Scandinavians, particularly Swedes, were well established in Ontario, with major settlements located in Thunder Bay, Kenora, and Toronto.

Those who went to the urban centres tended to set up shops and small manufacturing businesses.

The opening of the West attracted Scandinavian immigrants. Immigration, however, declined precipitously during the First World War, but rose in the years that followed until 1931, peaking in 1927 at just over 12,000. The United States had been the favoured destination for Scandinavian immigrants prior to the First World War. After the war, however, when the United States began to restrict immigration, Canada became the beneficiary (Figure 20).

FIGURE 20
Scandinavian immigration to Canada, 1900–66

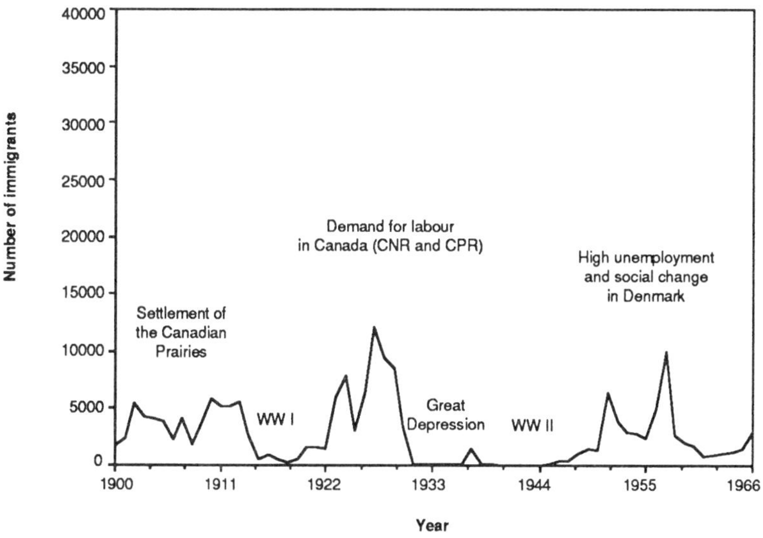

SOURCE: See Figure 5

The Great Depression and the Second World War slowed all immigration to Canada. When it resumed in 1947 a different kind of Scandinavian immigrant predominated. Most were well educated, employed in white-collar occupations, and preferred to settle in the urban centres of British Columbia and Ontario. Most of the postwar immigrants came for economic reasons. The late 1960s saw improvements in the economies of the Scandinavian countries and in their social conditions. This, along with a tightening of Canadian immigration regulations, significantly reduced the flow of immigrants to Canada. Scandinavians in Canada had increased from a population of 1,623 in 1871 to over 300,000 at the time of the 1971 Census. Their patterns of immigration and settlement during the twentieth century are reflected in their significantly high levels of relative concentration in the West compared to the East (Figure 21).

Ukrainian immigrants came in the 1890s, as part of the large influx of southern and eastern Europeans who came to Canada in response to Sifton's campaign to recruit immigrants. As indicated in Figure 22, many Ukrainians settled in bloc settlements along the southern edge of the Canadian Shield in Manitoba, Saskatchewan, and Alberta (Gerus and Rea 1985). By the time of the 1911 Census, Ukrainians numbered over 100,000.

The First World War brought Ukrainian immigration to a halt. It resumed in 1924 with the second wave which was composed of political refugees, ex-soldiers, university professors, and labourers, many of whom settled in Ontario (Gerus and Rea 1985:13). Ukrainian immigrants of this period were better educated and more 'nationally conscious' than were their predecessors, but, even so, many of the immigrants were farmers or farm labourers headed for the Prairies. It was during this period that Winnipeg became the cultural centre for Ukrainians in Canada (see Gerus and Rea 1985:12-3 and *Ontario Ethnocultural Profiles* on Ukrainians 1979).

The third wave took place from 1947 to the early 1950s and was largely composed of refugees, that is, individuals who had been displaced by war (Figure 22). Most of the immigrants were men, many of whom came to work in the forests and mines of northern Ontario. They were sponsored by mining and forestry companies that gave them eighteen-month contracts. As soon as their contracts were over most of the immigrants gravitated to the cities of southern Ontario, especially Toronto, which became the cultural centre of the third wave (Gerus and Rea 1985). Third-wave Ukrainians were more politically oriented than their predecessors. Included were the political elite, university-educated, individuals, skilled technologists, and professionals. These postwar refugees represented the end of significant Ukrainian immigration to Canada (Gerus and Rea 1985:18). According to the census, the Ukrainian population numbered 580,660 and was the fifth largest ethnic group in Canada in 1971.

Ukrainian patterns of immigration and settlement of the twentieth century are clearly reflected in Figure 23. By 1971 they were significantly overconcentrated in the West, in the urban centres of Ontario, and in the forestry and mining regions of Ontario, but were underconcentrated in the eastern provinces.

General impressions of ethnic concentrations gained from an examination of the maps can be made more precise with the quan-

FIGURE 21
Scandinavian origin population,
Canada, 1971

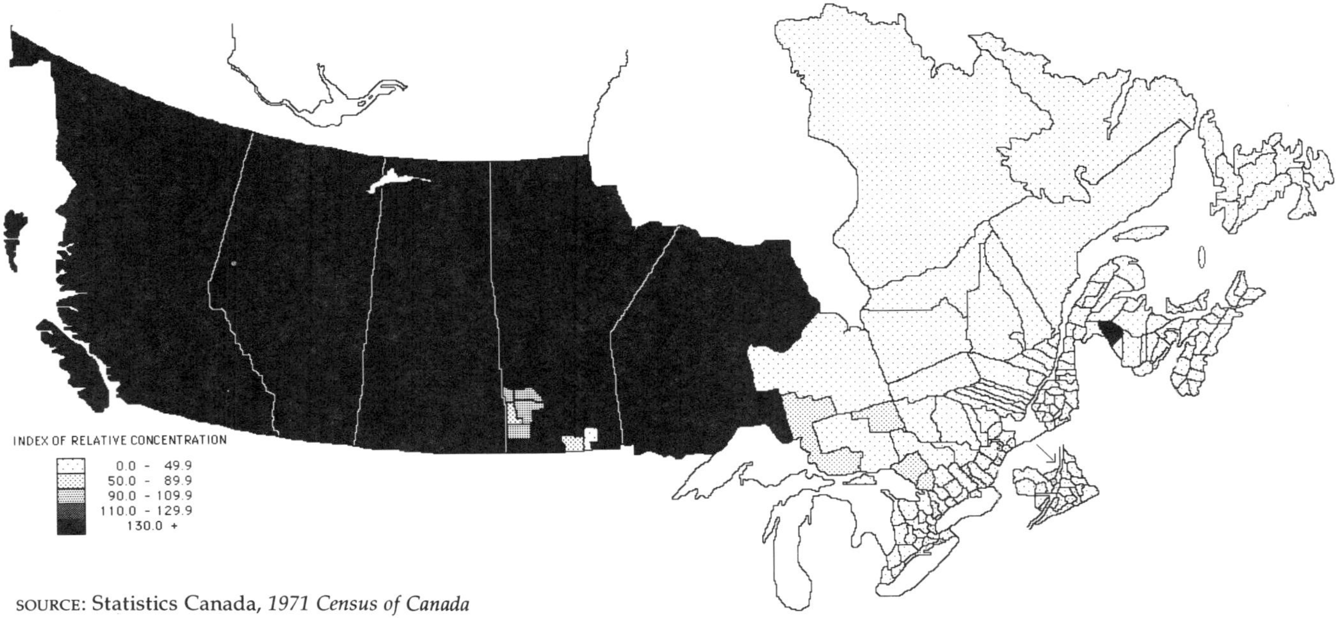

INDEX OF RELATIVE CONCENTRATION

0.0 – 49.9
50.0 – 89.9
90.0 – 109.9
110.0 – 129.9
130.0 +

SOURCE: Statistics Canada, *1971 Census of Canada*

FIGURE 22

Ukrainian immigration to Canada, 1900–66

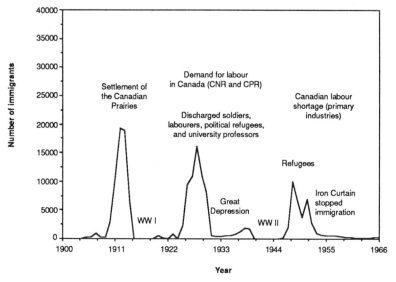

SOURCE: See Figure 3

titative index of dissimilarity (Table 2). The index of dissimilarity, which ranges from zero to one hundred, indicates the percentage of one population that would have to be relocated (to other census districts) to produce a distribution identical to that of some other population which has been selected as a reference population. Indexes for nine major ethnic populations have been calculated using the residential distribution of the English origin as the standard or reference population. The indexes of dissimilarity range from a low of 29.0 for the Irish origin population to a high of 81.7 for the French origin population. The individual British origin groups and other northern and western European origins, that is, German, Dutch, and Scandinavian, show the lowest degree of segregation from the English, with indexes ranging from 29 to about 47. The Italian and Polish exhibited fairly high indexes of 66.6 and 69.8, respectively.

These results are consistent with the findings of more recent research with respect to levels of ethnic segregation in Canada (Darroch and Marston 1969; Balakrishnan 1976; Kalbach 1981). The only exception was the French, who exhibited a significantly higher degree of segregation from the English in 1871 than in 1971.

In summation, it seems that because the English were the cultur-

FIGURE 23
Ukrainian origin population,
Canada, 1971

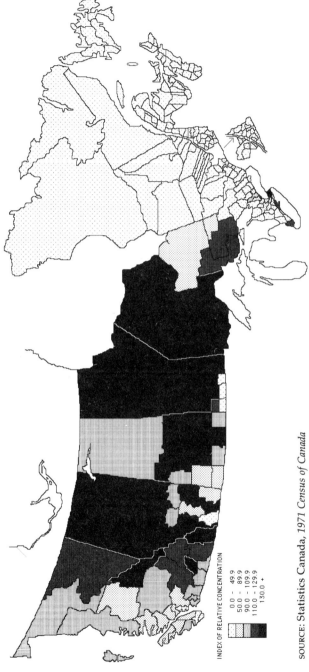

INDEX OF RELATIVE CONCENTRATION

0.0 - 49.9
50.0 - 89.9
90.0 - 109.9
110.0 - 129.9
130.0 +

SOURCE: Statistics Canada, 1971 *Census of Canada*

TABLE 2

Indexes of dissimilarity for selected ethnic origin populations,
Canada, 1871

Ethnic origin	Index of dissimilarity
English	Comparison population
Irish	29.0
Scottish	37.4
Welsh	32.2
French	81.7
German	47.4
Italian	66.6
Dutch	45.4
Polish	69.8
Scandinavian	46.5

SOURCE: *1871 Census of Canada*, Volume 1, Table III

ally and economically dominant group in Canada in 1871 and 1971, individuals belonging to the other ethnic groups would find them the most desirable as marriage partners compared to individuals belonging to the other groups. English patterns of relatively high concentration overlap to some extent with the other ethnic origin groups, except for the French, making them accessible as possible marriage partners. The Irish and the Scottish also tend to overlap to some extent with most of the other groups, so they too might be possible marriage partners if English spouses were unavailable.

This chapter discusses the immigration history and settlement patterns of the English, Irish, Scottish, French, German, Italian, Dutch, Polish, Scandinavian, and Ukrainian ethnic groups from their early days in Canada to 1971. The patterns exhibited by each group will have an effect on patterns of intermarriage in 1871 and 1971. The English, while not numerically dominant in the nineteenth century, were dominant culturally and economically, and therefore make the most attractive marriage partners to members of the other ethnic groups in Canada. This research suggests that intermarriage was a pathway to assimilation. Before this is explored, the socio-economic characteristics of the ethnic groups under study must be examined. It is known, for example, that levels of educational attainment, occupational attainment, religion, and urban/rural characteristics all influence propensities for intermarriage (Barron 1972:100–1). The task of the next chapter will be to examine these characteristics of each ethnic group in 1871 and 1971 as background to an analysis of patterns of intermarriage.

CHAPTER FOUR

Canada's Ethnic Populations

'Among the social variables affecting intermarriage incidence and direction are group size, sex ratio, age composition, and degree and kind of intergroup contact' (Barron 1972:11). Educational, occupational, and religious characteristics also affect the incidence and propensity for ethnic intermarriage (Barron 1972:43). The previous chapter suggests that intergroup contact among Canada's ethnic groups was somewhat limited in the nineteenth century compared to that of the twentieth century, at least in terms of the number of distinct ethnic or cultural groups with whom an individual might come in contact. By the time of the 1971 Census, data were reported for fifty-one distinct ethnic groups compared to only eighteen for the 1871 Census. Canada's urban/rural character also changed during the century. Increasing urbanization and residential mobility have increased the amount of interaction between all segments of Canada's population and the probability of intermarriage between a variety of ethnic and socio-economic groups.

This chapter examines the characteristics of Canada's ethnic populations with a view to providing insight into their patterns of ethno-religious intermarriage in 1871 and 1971. The characteristics considered are those shown in the literature to have an effect on those patterns. Religion, for example, has been shown to reinforce ethnic ties and would therefore be expected to inhibit marital assimilation by reinforcing ethnic endogamy for most groups. High levels of occupational and educational attainment have been shown to favour intermarriage, as has an imbalance in the sex ratio (number of males per one hundred females). Age and generation are also significantly related to intermarriage (Barron 1972:42–3; Merton 1972:15).

In essence this chapter will provide the base from which to begin the analysis of patterns of ethno-religious intermarriage in Canada in 1871 and 1971. It begins by examining the growth of ethnic populations in Canada and changes in religious composition between 1871 and 1971. Subsequent sections of the chapter will examine age-sex compositions, sex ratios, rural/urban distributions, marital status, and occupational and educational characteristics of the English, Irish, Scottish, French, Germans, Italians, Dutch, Polish, Scandinavians, and Ukrainians.

POPULATION TRENDS OF CANADA'S ETHNIC POPULATIONS

The discussion of ethnic groups in this research is based on the ethnic or cultural origin questions used in Canada's censuses. One question has been used throughout the years, permitting 'a rough but adequate delineation of the basic ethnic structure and its evolution through time' (Kalbach and McVey 1979:194).[1]

The ethnic or cultural character of Canadian society in 1971 had essentially been established by the time of the 1871 Census. The French and the politically dominant British were the founding charter groups. Immigration, however, was unable to continue drawing as heavily from these two primary cultural pools. Had it been able to do so Canada's population would not have been as diverse in 1971 as it was. The migration stream added people from many other cultures, and by 1971, taken together, they were rapidly approaching a size that might ultimately challenge the supremacy of the charter groups.[2] The importance of the non-charter groups is revealed by the fact that Canada proclaimed a policy of multiculturalism a few months after the 1971 Census.

The British are not a homogeneous group, and its individual ethnic components have varied in size. As previously noted, the Irish made up the largest component until the 1921 Census, when for the first time they were exceeded by the English and the Scottish, a position that has since been maintained. A comparison of the components of the British population reveals that the English and the Scottish grew at a faster rate than the Irish in every decade between 1871 and 1921 (Figure 24), and the rate of growth for the English origin population exceeded the rate for the Scottish. By 1961 the growth rate of the Irish and Scottish populations began to decline, while the English population's rate of growth showed a greater increase between 1961 and 1971 than in the four previous decades.

The rate of growth for those of French origin, dependent mainly on natural increase, was strikingly steady during the entire century.

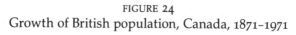

FIGURE 24
Growth of British population, Canada, 1871–1971

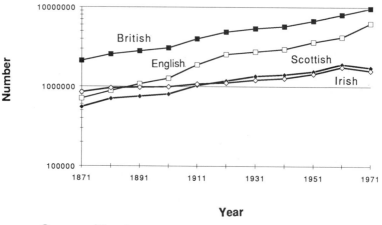

Year

SOURCE: Censuses of Canada

The population of British origin, however, was more dependent on immigration, and, therefore, its rate of growth was subject to more variation (Figures 24 and 25; see also Kalbach and McVey 1979: 195–7). The German, Dutch, Italian, and Polish origin populations all exhibited rapid and continuous growth throughout the century. There was some decline in growth experienced by all of the groups during the depression years, as would be expected, except for the Dutch. This can probably be explained by the fact that during the 1931–41 decade many Germans identified themselves as Dutch, that is, Deutsch, because it was undesirable to be 'German' (Ryder 1955:471–2). Growth rates increased again after the postwar years for each of the four ethnic populations (Figure 25).

The greatest increase in growth for the Italians occurred during the 1951–61 decade (Figure 25). By 1971 they exceeded the Polish and the Dutch in size, and ranked fourth overall. Ukrainians experienced their greatest increase in growth during the first decade of the twentieth century (Figure 26). Growth continued throughout the century but at a much slower rate during the postwar years, mainly due to the virtual cessation of Ukrainian immigration in the early 1950s (see Figure 22).

NATIVE-BORN AND FOREIGN-BORN COMPONENTS

The differences in the native-born and foreign-born components of ethnic groups reflect the relative contributions of net migration and

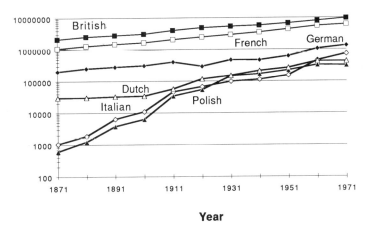

FIGURE 25
Growth of selected ethnic populations, Canada, 1871–1971

SOURCE: Censuses of Canada

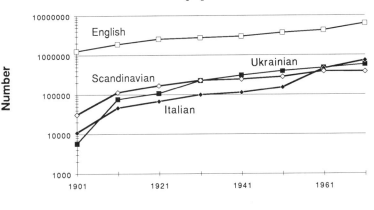

FIGURE 26
Growth of selected ethnic populations, Canada, 1901–71

SOURCE: Censuses of Canada

natural increase. Between 1871 and 1971 natural increase has been the primary factor in the growth of the French population, and it increased in importance for the English, Irish, and Scottish as immigration from the United Kingdom declined. The English native-born increased from 76.4 per cent in 1871 to 87.4 in 1971. The proportion of native-born Irish increased to 91.8 per cent in 1971 from only 71.8 per cent in 1871, while the native-born component of the Scottish increased from about 75 per cent in 1871 to 85 per cent in 1971. The native-born component of the French was already high in 1871 at 99.2 per cent, but due to declining fertility dropped slightly to 98.2 per cent by 1971 (Figures 27 and 28). The high proportions of native-born British and French limited the impact of immigration on Canadian society as a whole throughout the century.

Immigration has been a much more important factor for the growth of the Other European origins. During the Great Depression, however, when immigration almost ceased, the native born increased significantly (Kalbach and McVey 1979:214). By 1971, the native-born proportion of the total population had increased slightly to 84.7 per cent from just over 82 per cent in 1871.

RELIGIOUS COMPOSITION OF CANADA'S ETHNIC GROUPS

'Marriage patterns tend to support the existing religious structure' (Kalbach and McVey 1979:231). In 1971, for example, 61 per cent of all couples married were of the same denomination (Statistics Canada 1974:Table 14). Other research, however, indicates an increase in interfaith marriages between Protestants, Jews, and Catholics (Heer and Hubay 1975). Religion is an integral part of ethnic-connectedness (Alba and Golden 1986:217). Canadian census data provide a unique opportunity to examine backgrounds in both religion and ancestry.[3] The analysis begins with a description of the religious structure of the total population and each ethnic group in 1871 and 1971.

The census of 1871 shows that 41.8 per cent of the population were Roman Catholics, 16.3 per cent were Methodists, 15.8 per cent were Presbyterians, and 15 per cent were Anglicans. The next largest groups were Baptist, 'Other Religions,' Lutheran, and 'No Religion.' By 1971 the Roman Catholic denomination had increased its proportionate share to 46.2 per cent (Figure 29). In 1925, Methodists, Congregationalists, and Presbyterians merged to form the United Church of Canada, which ranked second in 1971 with 17.2 per cent. Not all Presbyterians became members of the United Church, but

FIGURE 27
Percentage distribution of ethnic groups by nativity, Canada, 1871

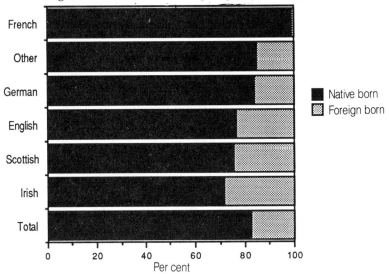

SOURCE: Canadian Historical Mobility Project, *1871 Census of Canada*

FIGURE 28
Percentage distribution of ethnic groups by nativity, Canada, 1971

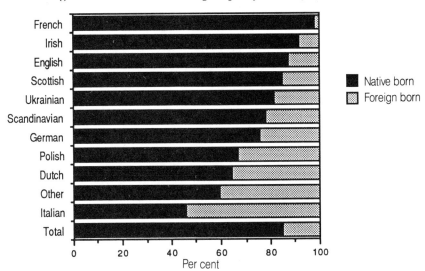

SOURCE: Statistics Canada, *1971 Census of Canada*, Special Tabulations

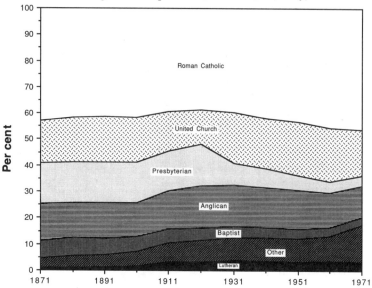

FIGURE 29

Religious composition, Canada, 1871–1971

Per cent

Roman Catholic

United Church

Presbyterian

Anglican

Baptist

Other

Lutheran

1871   1891   1911   1931   1951   1971

SOURCE: Censuses of Canada

NOTE: United Church refers to Methodists from 1871 to 1921

during the century this denomination lost ground. Baptists and Anglicans had also declined proportionately by 1971. Lutherans and Other denominations increased their proportions by 1971.

It can be seen that there is considerable variation in the religious composition of Canadian ethnic populations as reflected in their religious characteristics in 1871 and 1971 (Figures 30 and 31). In 1871 the English were predominantly Methodist and Anglican, while the Irish were mainly Protestant (Methodist and Anglican) with a significant proportion of Roman Catholics. The Scottish were primarily Presbyterian (Figure 30). At the time of the 1971 Census, data were only published for the British as a whole.[4] However, the religious composition of the British ethnic origin group tends to reflect the denominations of its three major components, namely, Irish Roman Catholics, Scottish Presbyterians, and English Anglicans and United Church (Figure 31).[5]

The French at both time periods and the Italians at the time of the 1971 Census were the most homogeneous of the ethnic populations with respect to religious composition. Over 90 per cent of the French in 1871 and 1971 reported themselves as Roman Catholic. Similarly, over 90 per cent of Italians reported themselves as being Roman Catholic in 1971. The Poles were also among the more religiously homogeneous groups in 1971, with just over 73 per cent reporting themselves as Roman Catholic.

FIGURE 30
Religious composition of ethnic groups, Canada, 1871

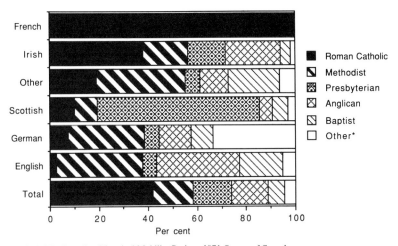

SOURCE: Canadian Historical Mobility Project, *1871 Census of Canada*
NOTE: *Includes Lutheran, No Religion and All Other

FIGURE 31
Religious composition of ethnic groups, Canada, 1971

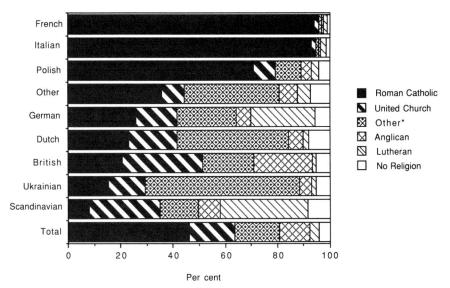

SOURCE: Statistics Canada, *1971 Census of Canada*
NOTE: *Includes Other Protestant, Ukrainian Orthodox, Ukrainian Catholic, and All Other

The German population presents an example of an ethnic population with two distinctive sub-cultural groups, that is, the German Roman Catholics and the German Lutherans in 1971 and the German Methodists and German Lutherans (as reflected in the size of the 'Other' category) in 1871. German Roman Catholics were not a major force in 1871, but by 1971 had increased their share to 25.7 per cent of the German population from only 7.6 per cent a century earlier. The Dutch exhibited a similar cultural bifurcation along religious lines at the time of the 1971 Census, with Other Dutch Protestants (falling under Other) and a significant proportion of Roman Catholics (Figure 31).

One of the factors affecting changes in religious composition is immigration. The proportion of foreign born belonging to Catholic denominations increased from 28 per cent in 1951 to 42 per cent by 1971 (Kalbach and McVey 1979:235). Between the 1961 and 1971 censuses the number of foreign born who reported themselves as Anglicans, Lutherans, and United Church actually declined. Baptists and Presbyterians increased, but not in sufficient numbers to increase their proportions of foreign born (ibid.). While increases in interfaith marriages in Canada have been noted (Heer and Hubay 1975), it remains to be seen whether there has been any increase in ethno-religious intermarriage, and what role religion, compared to the role of ethnic or cultural origin, plays in patterns of intermarriage.

The 1971 Census was the first time that it was possible to examine the multidimensional aspect of Canada's ethnic origin groups. Darroch and Ornstein's sample of approximately 10,000 households drawn from the 1871 Census (Canadian Historical Mobility Project) now makes it possible to examine these complexities and to compare them with the data collected a century later (Darroch 1986:5-14). Data on religious affiliation for selected ethnic origin groups for immigrants and the native born are presented in Table 3. While data for the foreign born do not necessarily reveal the religious affiliation of immigrants before coming to this country, the original religious affiliation is probably more closely reflected in the data for the first generation than it is in the data for the native born. Data for the native born would show the effects of assimilation, as well as the relative growth of subsequent generations.

In 1871 Anglicans comprised nearly half of the English foreign born, but did not have this dominance in the native-born population. Methodists had increased their share slightly among the native born, and Baptists showed the largest gains among the native-born English population (Table 3). Roman Catholics comprised 47 per cent

TABLE 3

Percentage distribution of religious denominations by ethnic origin and nativity, Canada, 1871 and 1971

1871

Ethnic origin and nativity	Roman Catholic	Anglican	Lutheran	Methodist	Presbyterian	Baptist	Other	Total Per cent	Total Number
English									
Foreign born	1.9	48.8	–	33.6	4.0	6.2	5.5	100.0	1,238
Native born	2.8	29.8	0.2	35.6	5.7	20.5	5.3	100.0	4,012
Irish									
Foreign born	47.4	21.9	–	14.7	13.2	1.4	1.4	100.0	1,727
Native born	34.3	22.9	–	19.8	15.9	5.1	2.0	100.0	4,395
Scottish									
Foreign born	4.5	2.9	–	6.6	78.9	4.6	2.5	100.0	943
Native born	11.8	6.2	0.0	10.5	61.6	6.5	3.3	100.0	2,888
French									
Foreign born	84.7	3.2	3.8	5.9	–	2.4	–	100.0	54
Native born	98.3	0.5	0.0	0.3	0.4	0.3	0.1	100.0	7,261
German									
Foreign born	10.7	8.7	38.3	21.2	6.7	2.4	12.0	100.0	246
Native born	7.0	13.9	13.3	32.9	5.5	10.3	17.1	100.0	1,256

(continued on next page)

TABLE 3 (continued)

Ethnic origin and nativity	Roman Catholic	Anglican	Lutheran	Methodist	Presbyterian	Baptist	Other	Total Per cent	Total Number
Other									
Foreign born	9.7	9.3	4.3	49.8	7.3	13.7	6.0	100.0	73
Native born	20.4	12.1	0.4	34.0	5.9	22.2	5.0	100.0	419
Total									
Foreign born	22.5	24.2	2.5	19.4	24.3	3.7	3.5	100.0	4,305
Native born	45.7	13.1	0.9	15.8	14.0	7.3	3.1	100.0	20,291

1971

Ethnic origin and nativity	Roman Catholic	Anglican	Lutheran	United Church	Presbyterian	Baptist	U. Cath. Gr. Ortho.	No Religion	Other	Total Per cent	Total Number
British											
Foreign born	14.2	35.8	0.9	17.7	13.8	3.7	0.1	7.7	6.2	100.0	11,858
Native born	21.3	20.7	1.4	33.0	6.6	5.3	0.2	5.2	6.3	100.0	83,029
French											
Foreign born	80.0	2.3	1.0	3.7	1.4	0.8	0.7	6.5	3.6	100.0	1,198
Native born	94.4	0.9	0.1	1.8	0.3	0.6	0.2	1.0	0.7	100.0	60,367
German											
Foreign born	27.3	2.5	36.2	6.8	1.5	4.0	0.3	5.8	15.4	100.0	3,277
Native born	25.3	6.5	20.5	19.2	2.6	4.4	0.3	5.0	16.2	100.0	9,972

Italian											
Foreign born	96.9	0.3	0.1	0.4	0.2	0.1	0.2	0.8	1.1	100.0	3,944
Native born	90.2	2.0	0.3	3.1	0.6	0.4	0.2	1.7	1.6	100.0	3,319
Dutch											
Foreign born	26.7	2.6	2.4	12.6	5.3	2.1	–	12.6	35.6	100.0	1,493
Native born	20.4	7.4	1.8	20.6	4.5	3.7	–	7.3	34.3	100.0	2,830
Polish											
Foreign born	80.7	1.2	3.5	2.7	0.6	0.9	3.9	4.0	2.6	100.1	1,040
Native born	63.9	5.3	2.9	12.5	1.8	1.0	3.7	4.9	4.0	100.0	2,083
Scandinavian											
Foreign born	3.2	4.8	58.0	11.2	2.8	2.2	0.6	8.2	9.1	100.0	785
Native born	9.3	8.8	26.2	31.6	2.3	2.8	0.4	9.2	9.4	100.0	2,903
Ukrainian											
Foreign born	7.8	1.1	0.8	3.9	0.5	1.2	77.2	4.5	3.1	100.0	1,055
Native born	16.6	5.6	1.8	16.1	1.8	1.8	46.2	5.6	4.4	100.0	4,891
Other											
Foreign born	36.9	2.9	6.4	4.0	2.1	1.4	14.5	8.6	23.1	100.0	8,348
Native born	34.2	9.6	4.0	12.3	2.3	2.0	5.6	6.8	23.1	100.0	11,627
Total											
Foreign born	35.7	14.2	7.2	9.3	6.1	2.3	6.4	6.9	11.9	100.0	32,998
Native born	48.1	11.3	2.6	19.0	3.6	3.2	1.8	4.0	6.4	100.0	181,021

SOURCE: 1871: Canadian Historical Mobility Project, *1871 Census of Canada*; 1971: Statistics Canada, *1971 Census of Canada*, Public Use Sample, Individual File

of the Irish foreign born, but just over one-third of the Irish native born. It would appear that they lost ground to Methodists, Presbyterians, and Baptists, all of whom gained in their proportionate share of the native-born Irish. These gains resulted in greater religious heterogeneity among the native-born population. The Scottish were more homogeneous with respect to religion in 1871 than were the English or the Irish. Nearly 79 per cent of the Scottish foreign born were Presbyterian, as were 61.9 per cent of the native-born Scots. Each of the other denominations among the native born gained at the expense of the Presbyterians, especially the Roman Catholic and Methodist denominations (Table 3). This may be a reflection of marital assimilation in that some Scots may have married spouses who were either English or Irish Methodists, or Irish Roman Catholic.

The French population, both native- and foreign-born, was the most religiously homogeneous of any of the ethnic groups in 1871. Roman Catholics comprised 98 per cent of the native-born French population, an increase from about 85 per cent for the foreign born. In contrast, the German population was the most heterogeneous in terms of their religious characteristics. In this case, the proportions of their native born who were affiliated with their ethnic denominations (Lutheran and Roman Catholic) had decreased to 13.9 and 7.0 per cent, respectively, from 38.3 and 10.7 per cent for their foreign born. The major Canadian churches showed significant gains among the native-born generations vis-à-vis the foreign-born generation (Table 3). This likely reflects either the willingness of native-born Germans to marry across religious lines or a shortage of partners claiming Lutheran as their affiliation.

One hundred years later, Roman Catholics were still dominant among the French native and foreign born. While the proportion of Roman Catholics is slightly less for both native born and foreign born compared to 1871, it is still extremely high at 80 per cent for the foreign born and just over 94 per cent for the native born (Table 3). Similarly, Roman Catholics were predominant among the Italian foreign- and native-born populations in 1971. The slight decline in the proportion of Roman Catholics in the native-born Italian population and the slight gains by the Canadian churches, that is, Anglican and United Church, may be a reflection of marital assimilation.

The Ukrainians were one of the most heterogeneous groups shown in Table 3. Among those who were foreign born, 48 per cent were Ukrainian Catholic and another 29 per cent were Greek Orthodox. Among the native born, the two religious groups only accounted for 46 per cent in contrast to 77 per cent for the foreign born. Sixteen per cent reported United Church and just over 16 per cent were Roman Catholic.

AGE AND SEX COMPOSITION

A radical imbalance in the sex ratio, that is, number of males per hundred females, exerts a pressure for intermarriage (Hurd 1929:24-5; Merton 1972:15). Table 4 presents the proportions of males and females for ethnic groups in 1871 and 1971. One would not

TABLE 4

Percentage distribution of the population by ethnic group and sex, Canada, 1871 and 1971

	1871			
	Total			
Ethnic origin	Number	Per cent	Male	Female
English	5,271	100.0	52.2	47.8
Irish	6,131	100.0	49.5	50.5
Scottish	3,834	100.0	50.4	49.6
French	7,329	100.0	50.0	50.0
German	1,514	100.0	50.9	49.1
Other	497	100.0	48.0	52.0
Total	24,567	100.0	50.4	49.6

	1971			
English	6,245,975	100.0	49.0	51.0
Irish	1,581,725	100.0	50.4	49.6
Scottish	1,720,390	100.0	50.4	49.6
French	6,180,120	100.0	49.8	50.2
German	1,317,195	100.0	50.7	49.3
Italian	730,820	100.0	52.5	47.5
Dutch	425,925	100.0	51.6	48.4
Polish	316,430	100.0	51.3	48.7
Scandinavian	384,790	100.0	51.8	48.2
Ukrainian	580,660	100.0	50.9	49.1
Other	2,084,260	100.0	51.5	48.5
Total	21,568,310	100.0	50.1	49.9

SOURCE: Canadian Historical Mobility Project, *1871 Census of Canada*; Statistics Canada, *1971 Census of Canada*, Special Tabulations

expect sex ratios to have much affected patterns of intermarriage in 1871, since the distributions of ethnic groups by sex were not radically disproportionate. The possible exceptions might be for those of English and Other origins. The data for 1971 reveal a similar picture, with the possible exception of the Dutch, Polish, Scandin-avians, and those of Other cultural origins. In general, however, it is clear that males outnumber females for most groups in both time periods, and this fact would likely have some effect on patterns of ethno-religious intermarriage.

The actual sex ratios for ethnic groups in 1871 and 1971 are given in Table 5. Kalbach and McVey note that 'historically, the sex ratio has reflected an almost constant excess of male births (about 106 males per 100 female births), and until recently males tended to outnumber females in immigrant populations' (1979:158). In 1871 this was true for all ethnic groups except the Irish and those of Other origins. By 1971 there had been a decline in the ratio of males to females for the English, Irish, French, and Germans, with the Scottish remaining about the same. The greatest excess of males for any group was recorded for the English in 1871 and the Italians in 1971. The more recent immigrant groups all exhibited an excess of

TABLE 5

Number of males per 100 females for selected ethnic populations, Canada, 1871 and 1971

Ethnic origin	1871	1971
English	109.2	96.1
Irish	97.9	101.7
Scottish	101.8	101.7
French	100.0	99.1
German	103.5	102.9
Italian	–	110.7
Dutch	–	106.7
Polish	–	105.7
Scandinavian	–	107.4
Ukrainian	–	103.8
Other	92.3	106.2
Total	101.7	100.4

SOURCE: Canadian Historical Mobility Project, *1871 Census of Canada*; Statistics Canada, *1971 Census of Canada*, Special Tabulations
NOTE: Dash indicates that data is unavailable.

male over females in 1971 (Table 5). The variations in the sex ratios suggest differential rates of intermarriage.

More generally one can consider the age-sex composition of the ethnic populations in 1871 and 1971, since both affect the likelihood of intermarriage. Population pyramids graphically display a population's age and sex composition. They show proportions of males and females in five-year age groups, usually up to seventy-five years of age and older. The sum of the percentages for all the age-sex groupings of a population is shown as 100 per cent. An age-sex pyramid also graphically portrays the consequence of earlier fertility, mortality, and immigration experience. A broad base, for example, reflects high fertility. In addition, there is generally a slightly larger number of males because there are about 106 males born for every 100 females. A constricted base reflects shrunken birth cohorts as a result of declining fertility rates. As cohorts age, they inevitably lose members due to mortality, and they may either gain or lose because of migration.

Canada's population shows the result of higher levels of fertility in 1871 compared to 1971 (Figure 32). The obvious effects of declining fertility and an excess of males due to immigration are apparent in the pyramid for Canada's population at the time of the 1971 Census. An examination of age-sex pyramids for specific ethnic groups in 1871 and 1971 reveals similar patterns in that the English, Irish, Scottish, French, German, and Other origins all show evidence of high rates of growth in 1871 (Figure 33) and declining growth rates in 1971 (Figure 34). The effects of a heavier immigration of males compared to females is apparent in all of the pyramids for 1871.

Like sex ratios, the age composition of Canada's ethnic populations varied, and for many of the same reasons. Those groups experiencing high fertility and some immigration exhibit both high proportions of their populations in the younger age groups and smoothly tapered pyramids, much like those of the French and English in 1871. The Scottish and the Irish experiences of high fertility and heavy immigration prior to 1871 are reflected by the high proportions in the youngest age groups and the overabundance of males in the older populations (60+). By 1971 the English, Irish, and Scottish showed the effects of low fertility, low mortality, and declining immigration, while evidence of declining fertility during the 1960s is reflected in the narrowing of the base of the pyramid for the French.

In 1971 the Dutch exhibited a similar pattern to the French. The overabundance of males in the older populations, however, reflects

FIGURE 32
Age and sex composition, Canada, 1871 and 1971

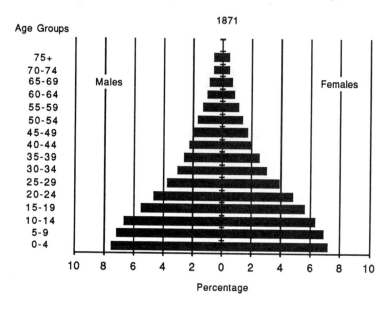

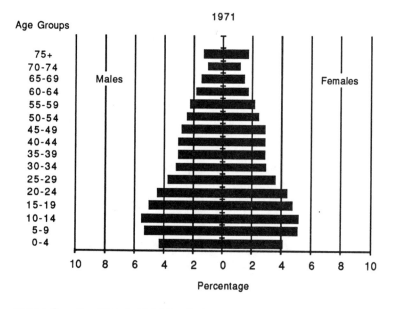

SOURCE: Canadian Historical Mobility Project, *1871 Census of Canada*; Statistics Canada, *1971 Census of Canada*, Special Tabulations

FIGURE 33
Age and sex composition of selected ethnic origins, Canada, 1871

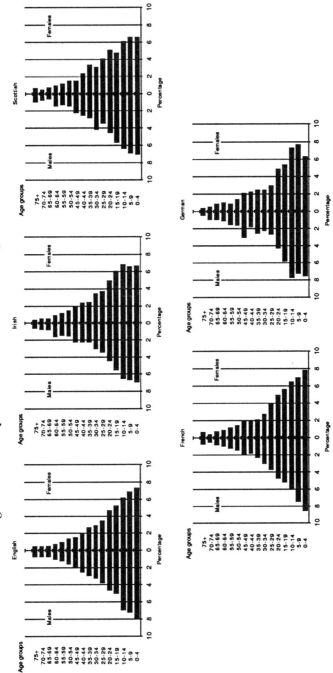

SOURCE: Canadian Historical Mobility Project, *1871 Census of Canada*

FIGURE 34
Age and sex composition of selected ethnic origins, Canada, 1971

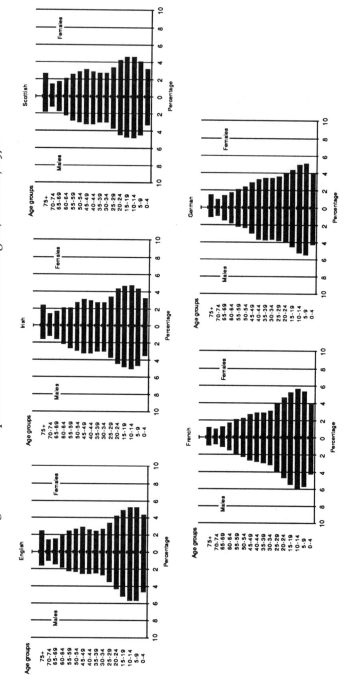

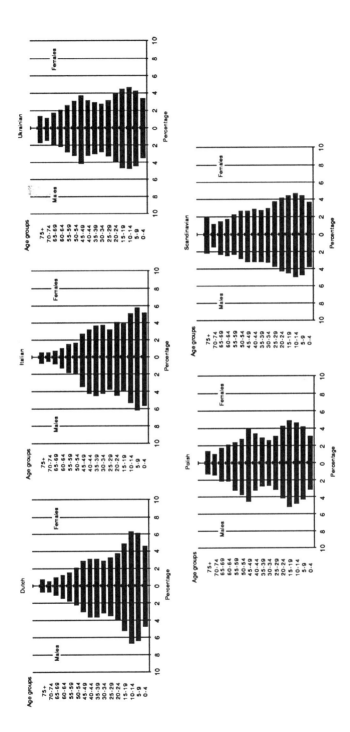

SOURCE: Statistics Canada, *1971 Census of Canada*, Special Tabulations

their immigration pattern of the early twentieth century. High fertility and sustained immigration throughout the nineteenth century is evident for the Germans in 1871, and the continuation of relatively strong immigration throughout the twentieth century is illustrated in the 1971 pyramid.

The Italian pattern of heavy immigration for limited periods during the twentieth century is reflected in the heavy concentrations in the young adult age groups (30-49) and the high proportions of children (0-9). Ukrainians show an excess of older males – survivors from the early 1900s immigration – and relatively high proportions in the older age groups. A similar pattern is revealed for the Poles and Scandinavians in 1971. Both populations show evidence of low fertility and a slow-down in immigration.

While these population pyramids are of interest in their own right, they also have implications for patterns of ethnic intermarriage. The 1871 pyramids suggest that the pressure for outmarriage would be greatest for those groups like the Irish, Scottish, and German, since they have an overabundance of males in the younger marriageable age groups (15-34). The pressure for intermarriage would be less likely among the French, as evidenced by their more even distribution of males and females in the young adult ages. The 1971 pyramids for the more recent groups, Italians, Ukrainians, Dutch, Scandinavians, and Poles reveal large excesses of males, which also suggests that a propensity for intermarriage for these groups is likely.

RURAL-URBAN VARIATIONS

The distribution of ethnic populations by urban and rural residence has implications for intermarriage. It is expected that, all other things being equal, individuals living in urban areas would be more likely to intermarry than those who live in rural areas (Hurd 1929:133). The pattern of immigrant settlement is also associated with the pace of urbanization in Canada. Thus, most of the immigrants have gravitated toward the large urban centres, bringing more diverse groups into contact with one another and enhancing the chances of intermarriage.

Certain ethnic groups, such as the Italians and Poles, have been predominantly urban, while others, like the Ukrainians and Dutch, have been predominantly rural. Canada was only 22 per cent urban in 1871 compared to nearly 76 per cent in 1971 (Figures 35 and 36). The Dutch were the most rural in 1871, followed by the German, Scottish, Other, and French origin populations. In 1971, the Dutch

FIGURE 35
Percentage distribution of ethnic groups by rural and urban
residence, Canada, 1871

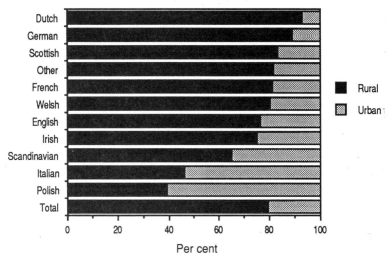

SOURCE: DBS, *1931 Census of Canada*, Ottawa: King's Printer 1936, Vol. 1, Table 35, p. 710

FIGURE 36
Percentage distribution of ethnic groups by rural and urban
residence, Canada, 1971

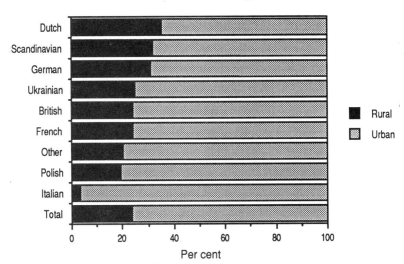

SOURCE: Statistics Canada, *1971 Census of Canada*, Bulletin 1.3-2, Ottawa: Information
Canada 1973

origin population was still the most rural, followed by the Scandinavians, Germans, and Ukrainians. Interestingly, the most urban groups at the time of the 1871 Census were the Poles and Italians, positions they still held in 1971. Thus, one would expect the latter to have been subject to an urban tendency toward intermarriage.

MARITAL STATUS

There is some evidence that individuals who have been married previously are more likely to intermarry than are those who have not (Barron 1972:44). The high proportions married (and widowed) in 1871 reflect a known tendency for early and frequent remarriage in historical populations (Nett 1981; Katz, Doucet, and Stern 1982:290). Taken alone this tendency might well have fostered greater intermarriage, other conditions being equal, than twentieth-century marital patterns. While it is not possible to determine from census data whether individuals have been previously married, it is useful to examine the variations in marital status of ethnic populations in Canada in 1871 and 1971. In both time periods the majority of individuals fifteen years of age and over were married. The proportion married of the total population over fifteen, however, decreased from 79.7 per cent in 1871 to 61.8 per cent in 1971. Similarly, the proportion married for each ethnic origin population declined between 1871 and 1971. Conversely, of course, the proportion single increased dramatically over one hundred years (Table 6).

OCCUPATIONAL AND EDUCATIONAL CHARACTERISTICS

High levels of educational and occupational attainment are associated with intermarriage (Barron 1972:43). Changes in these characteristics between 1871 and 1971 have been significant. The 1871 sample of census data indicates that 49.7 per cent of the population were classified as farmers, 17.4 per cent were engaged in semi-skilled and skilled occupations, and 16.5 per cent were artisans (Table 7). Professionals comprised 9.0 per cent of the labour force in 1871, while the remaining 4.9 per cent were servants and 2.5 per cent were working in clerical and related occupations.[6] Similar patterns of occupational distribution were exhibited by the Germans, French, and Irish. The high social and economic status of the English in 1871 is reflected in the higher proportions of professionals, managers, and artisans compared to the other ethnic populations. The Scottish also had higher levels of occupational status than the Irish, French, or Germans.

TABLE 6
Marital status by ethnic origin, in the population 15 years of age
and over, Canada, 1871 and 1971

1871

Ethnic origin	Single	Married	Widowed	Divorced	Separated	Total Per cent	Total Number
English	11.5	81.0	7.6	–	–	100.0	2,140
Irish	13.6	77.1	9.3	–	–	100.0	2,389
Scottish	13.9	76.4	9.8	–	–	100.0	1,492
French	10.3	82.1	7.5	–	–	100.0	2,817
German	10.2	83.0	6.7	–	–	100.0	569
Other	11.9	79.3	8.9	–	–	100.0	221
Total	12.0	79.7	8.3	–	–	100.0	9,627

1971

	Single	Married	Widowed	Divorced	Separated	Per cent	Number
British	26.7	61.7	7.4	1.6	2.6	100.0	67,550
French	32.7	58.9	5.2	0.6	2.6	100.0	42,577
German	23.6	67.1	5.9	1.5	1.9	100.0	9,388
Italian	23.3	70.7	4.0	0.6	1.4	100.0	4,885
Dutch	25.9	68.0	3.3	0.9	1.9	100.0	2,793
Polish	27.0	61.4	6.1	1.9	3.5	99.9	2,383
Scandinavian	25.5	64.4	6.0	1.6	2.7	100.0	2,711
Ukrainian	25.0	64.1	6.6	1.6	2.7	100.0	4,465
Other	28.0	61.8	6.1	1.5	2.6	100.0	14,046
Total	28.1	61.8	6.3	1.3	2.5	100.0	150,798

SOURCE: Canadian Historical Mobility Project, *1871 Census of Canada*; Statistics Canada, *1971 Census of Canada*, Public Use Sample Tape, Individual File
NOTES: Dashes indicate that data are unavailable. Ns for 1971 are sample Ns from the 1 per cent sample.

During the century, of course, urbanization and industrialization dramatically affected Canadian lifestyles and standards of living. The proportion of farmers dropped from 49.7 per cent to 6.1 per cent in 1971, with expansion of the non-agricultural sectors of the economy (Table 8). Similarly, each ethnic origin group experienced a decline in the proportions who were engaged in farming occupations over the century. While data for the English, Irish, and Scottish as distinct groups were unavailable in 1971, it is possible to look at

TABLE 7

Occupation by ethnic origin, Canada, 1871

Occupation	English	Irish	Scottish	French	German	Other	Total
Professional and managerial	11.6	8.6	9.5	8.2	6.1	4.7	9.0
Clerical and related occupations	3.4	2.2	2.2	2.2	2.3	2.0	2.5
Artisans	21.8	16.8	16.9	13.4	11.1	13.7	16.5
Semi-skilled and skilled	15.7	18.2	10.5	20.0	19.0	38.0	17.4
Servants	3.4	6.6	4.3	5.2	3.5	5.1	4.9
Farmers	44.2	47.7	56.6	51.1	58.0	36.4	49.7
Total (per cent)	100.1	100.1	100.0	100.1	100.0	99.9	100.0
(number)	1,464	1,768	1,072	1,896	395	135	6,730

SOURCE: Canadian Historical Mobility Project, 1871 Census of Canada

TABLE 8
Occupation by ethnic origin, Canada, 1971

Occupation	British	French	German	Italian	Dutch	Polish	Scandinavian	Ukrainian	Other	Total
Professional and managerial	18.7	14.9	14.7	6.8	13.8	14.1	16.2	13.1	17.5	16.5
Clerical and sales	28.8	22.8	23.0	17.8	20.3	21.4	23.1	23.1	23.0	25.3
Service	11.0	11.6	10.7	12.9	11.0	13.3	10.9	12.4	13.5	11.5
Farming	5.6	4.3	12.4	1.6	16.5	8.4	12.1	13.5	4.8	6.1
Skilled and semi-skilled	26.9	35.1	30.4	51.8	29.7	34.0	28.1	29.0	30.0	30.7
Occupation not stated	9.1	11.3	8.7	9.0	8.7	8.8	9.7	8.9	11.2	9.8
Total (per cent)	100.1	100.0	99.9	99.9	100.0	100.0	100.1	100.0	100.0	99.9
(number)	44,578	25,731	6,652	3,528	2,013	1,643	1,916	3,074	9,495	98,630

SOURCE: Statistics Canada, 1971 Census of Canada, Public Use Sample Tape, Individual File

the groups combined, that is, as British. The British still exhibited the highest proportions in white-collar occupations compared to the other ethnic groups in 1971, reflecting their economic dominance and their relatively higher status.

The Germans exhibit similar patterns in terms of their proportions in the white-collar occupations in comparison to the French and the British. The major difference is in the proportion of German (and Dutch) farmers and farm workers and reflects their role in the early settlement of Canada's Prairies. Italians, representative of Canada's postwar immigrants, reflect the time when many incoming immigrants were semi-skilled and unskilled workers. The characteristics of the Other ethnic origin category are reflective of immigration policy during the 1960s, which stressed education and occupational skills (Table 8).[7]

As previously noted, high levels of education also tend to influence patterns of intermarriage. Education in Canada did not become important until the last half of the nineteenth century, when major national school systems expanded throughout Europe and then North America (Synge 1976:402–4). Educational institutions were gradually built, and school attendance became compulsory, and even more importance was placed on education throughout the twentieth century. The early censuses collected data regarding school attendance and whether a person could read and write. A person who could do both was considered fully literate (elementary reading ability was more common than writing ability). Later censuses collected data on level of schooling attained, as well as school attendance. While literacy is not a measure of educational attainment per se, it is the only measure available for 1871. In essence, the 1871 Census data on an individual's ability to read and write represent a measure of basic literacy (UN 1965:704; Sills 1968:412–5). Table 9 reveals the percentage distribution of the population fifteen years of age and over by ethnic group and level of literacy in 1871. It can be seen that 20 per cent of the population fifteen years of age and older reported that they could not read and write and therefore, by the definition used in this research, were illiterate. In contrast, only 6 per cent of the population were illiterate in 1971.[8]

The table also reveals that in 1871 the high total illiteracy rate largely reflected the continued huge illiteracy of the French origin group. Fully 44 per cent of the French could not read or write. Although there is still limited historical research, in part, the high rate seems to have resulted from the fact that boys often left school at an early age to work on the family farm, and girls were only 'slightly' more likely to attend school than boys. In addition, school-

TABLE 9
Percentage of the population 15 years of age and over that is
illiterate, by ethnic origin, Canada, 1871 and 1971

Ethnic origin	1871 Per cent illiterate	1971 Per cent illiterate
British	9.9	3.3
English	6.1	–
Irish	11.9	–
Scottish	11.4	–
French	43.8	8.2
German	10.7	4.3
Italian	–	15.8
Dutch	–	2.3
Polish	–	9.5
Scandinavian	–	1.9
Ukrainian	–	13.4
Other	29.6	11.2
Total (per cent)	20.2	6.3
(number)	14,333	150,798

SOURCE: Canadian Historical Mobility Project, *1871 Census of Canada*; Statistics Canada,
  1971 Census of Canada, Public Use Sample, Individual File
NOTE: Dashes indicate that data are unavailable

ing in Quebec was not compulsory at the turn of the century or even
thirty-five years later (Miner 1939:35–37). The English were the most
literate of the specific ethnic populations, again reflecting their
social and economic dominance. Scandinavians were among the
most literate of the immigrant populations during the twentieth
century along with the Dutch and Germans, while the Ukrainians
and Italians were among the most illiterate (Hurd 1929:28). The data
presented in Table 9 support Hurd's earlier findings. These data
further suggest that those willing to intermarry in 1871 would most
likely prefer an English spouse or one of British origin in 1971. Their
higher levels of status from both an occupational and educational
view would make them more desirable as marriage partners than
those of other ethnic or cultural origin groups.

SUMMARY

Intermarriage is a reflection of both structural and normative or cultural factors (Merton 1972; Stevens and Swicegood 1987). This chapter examines some of the relevant characteristics that can be derived from historical and contemporary census data such as religious affiliation, nativity, education, sex ratios, rural/urban distribution, occupational status, age-sex composition, and marital status. The evidence and statistical base provides a unique perspective on Canada's social and demographic history – a perspective on which to build an analysis of the patterns of ethno-religious intermarriage in Canada just after Confederation and one hundred years later.

The analysis in this chapter revealed the importance of immigration for the cultural composition of Canada. Many individuals from cultural pools other than Britain and France were added to the Canadian mosaic, but, overall, the foreign-born population only experienced a slight increase between 1871 and 1971. As the character of the immigrant stream changed it included more and more groups belonging to Catholic denominations, such as Italians, Poles, and Ukrainians. The ethnic-connectedness of these groups due to their Catholic connection is expected to be much stronger than for some of the other groups (such as the Germans, Dutch, and Scandinavians) and is likely to result in lower propensities to intermarry, especially across religious lines. The strong rural character of the early Ukrainians and Poles, along with their tendency to settle in bloc settlements in the West, also suggests lower propensities for ethno-religious intermarriage. Urban immigrants, on the other hand, would likely have relatively high propensities for intermarriage by virtue of their propinquity to a wider variety of ethnic and cultural origin groups, particularly in 1971. An examination of sex-ratios and age-sex distributions for the various ethnic groups reveals an excess of males for almost all of them. The considerable variation across groups will likely have differential effects on patterns of ethno-religious intermarriage. Nineteenth-century patterns of age-sex composition and the greater likelihood of remarriage are likely to increase the probability of intermarriage to a greater extent than are twentieth-century patterns. On the other hand, the occupational and educational characteristics of twentieth-century immigrants are more likely to favour intermarriage than is the less rigid nature of occupational and educational status of the nineteenth century.

In summary, it is clear that the British group or its components, especially the English, would be the most desirable ethnic origin group from the point of view of intermarriage. Their cultural and economic dominance is reflected in their levels of literacy, higher levels of occupational attainment, and their affiliation with the

Anglican Church. In addition to the initial formal status, the Anglican Church is also more closely related to the Catholic denominations than are other denominations, and this may have proved attractive. It is likely, then, that higher proportions of individuals belonging to the other ethnic origins would probably choose English spouses if they intermarried. The next chapter examines patterns of intermarriage to see to what extent they differ between ethnic groups and to see how and to what extent some of the characteristics discussed in this chapter influence the patterns observed in Canada in 1871 and 1971.

CHAPTER FIVE

Prevalence and Patterns of Intermarriage in Canada, 1871 and 1971

Previous chapters have demonstrated that Canada has been shaped by immigration, fertility differences, changes in marital behaviour, and the population distribution across the country in the process of its continuing industrialization and urbanization. The objective of this chapter is to examine the prevalence and patterns of intermarriage in Canada at the time of the 1871 and 1971 censuses. It is known that both ethnic and religious intermarriage increased in Canada between 1921 and 1971 (Kalbach 1983:196–212). Ethnic differentials in patterns of intermarriage and between generations were also noted in virtually every study of intermarriage. Furthermore, religion was found to inhibit marital assimilation by reinforcing ethnic endogamy for most groups. In addition, assimilation theory points to the importance of the multidimensional nature of ethnicity, including cultural origin and religion. The two are so closely intertwined that each has some effect on the other.

Four questions arise from these findings. In the first place, what were the patterns of ethnic intermarriage that prevailed in the early years of Confederation? Second, is there a substantially greater general tendency toward intermarriage in the twentieth century? A positive answer to the second question is expected, especially in view of the fact that length of residence tends to be positively associated with increases in marital assimilation. Third, what were the differentials in the rates between ethnic groups in each century and between the two different periods of time? Fourth, was religion an apparent inhibitor of marital assimilation in both centuries? It is expected that it did in fact operate to limit intermarriage to a less extent in 1971. A multidimensional definition of ethnicity will be employed to answer this question.

This chapter examines the prevalence and patterns of intermarriage in 1871 and 1971. It looks first at the rates and patterns of ethnic exogamy expressed as percentages. Propensities for ethnic intermarriage will then be presented in order to refine the measurement of intermarriage by partially taking the size and sex ratio of the groups into account. A further refinement will be added by considering the multidimensional nature of ethnicity. Ethnicity in this case will be based on selected combinations of ethnic origin and religion and will be referred to as ethno-religious origins. The analysis will seek to determine the patterns of ethnic intermarriage for husbands of the selected ethno-religious origin groups.

A further refinement is considered. Ethno-religious marriages will be broken down into four categories of marital types. These four types range from marriages where husband and wife have different ethnic origins and different religious affiliations to the other end of the continuum where their ethnic origins and religious denominations are the same. Thus, the most assimilated are taken to be totally exogamous, while the least assimilated are totally endogamous with respect to ethnicity and religion. The rest are either the same ethnically but different in religion or of the same religion but different ethnicities, and occupy intermediate positions. It is hypothesized that a greater proportion of husbands will cross ethnic lines compared to religious lines or both ethnic and religious lines.

For the most part the data will be analysed for all husbands, as well as for native- and foreign-born husbands taken separately. The generational distinction is important because a high proportion of twentieth-century immigrants were married before they arrived in Canada (Kalbach 1970: Chart 2.20). While this may not necessarily have been the case for nineteenth-century immigrants, it is known that women were sometimes brought from the homeland as potential wives for the single unmarried males who came to settle the Canadian frontier. In any event, immigration generally tended to favour unattached males who might elect to outmarry if there was a shortage of females belonging to their ethnic or ethno-religious origin. This problem is less severe for those groups with a high proportion of native born, such as the French. Finding marriage partners was a serious problem for groups like the Irish in 1871 and the Italians in 1971, which are comprised of a large proportion of foreign born. Thus, the extrapolation of the native- and foreign-born components is important if one is to obtain a more precise measure of the propensity to outmarry.

ETHNIC INTERMARRIAGE

Patterns of ethnic intermarriage for native-born, foreign-born, and all husbands in 1871 are shown in Table 10. The data reveal that of the 3,757 husbands of husband-wife families, 82.9 per cent married spouses of the same ethnic origin, while 17.1 per cent married interethnically. Some variation between ethnic groups in terms of their tendency to marry within their own ethnic group is also revealed. In 1871 proportions of endogamy are highest for the French and Irish (96.7 and 82.9 per cent), which is not surprising given that they were numerically the two largest groups at that time and adherents to the Roman Catholic Church. The percentages were lowest for the smaller numerical groups, that is, English, Germans, and Others. Overall, however, English, Irish, Scottish, French, German, and Other husbands were overwhelmingly endogamous in 1871.

As argued above, an examination of the data by nativity provides a more precise measure of the propensity to intermarry. Data for native-born husbands of husband-wife families in 1871 reveal the persistence of high levels of endogamy for the English and French (73.0 and 96.9 per cent). Similar results are revealed for all native-born husbands combined. Considerably lower levels of endogamy, however, are exhibited by native-born husbands of Irish, Scottish, German, and Other ethnic origins. Also worthy of note, is the the change in rank order of the ethnic groups in terms of their tendency toward ethnic endogamy. The French still rank first, the Irish second, and the Scottish third, but the relative positions of all the other groups are different.

Data for foreign-born husbands indicate that, as expected, the majority of foreign-born husbands were more endogamous than their native-born counterparts in 1871. Only in the cases of the French and English did the native-born husbands exhibit a higher level of ethnic endogamy than the foreign-born husbands. The relatively small N for this group, however, suggests that caution should be exercised when interpreting the results. Nevertheless, it seems likely that the foreign-born French could have found wives of French origin, if they wished, given the numerical dominance of the native-born French population in Quebec; elsewhere in Canada finding a wife of French origin would be more problematic.

Table 11 shows patterns of ethnic intermarriage for native-born, foreign-born, and all husbands of husband-wife families in 1971. The data reveal that, of the 4,605,490 husbands, 62.7 per cent married wives of the same ethnic origin while 37.3 per cent married intereth-

TABLE 10

Percentage distribution of ethnically endogamous and exogamous marriages by ethnic origin and nativity of husband, Canada, 1871

Ethnic origin of husband	All husbands				Native-born husbands				Foreign-born husbands			
	Endoga-mous	Exoga-mous	Per cent	Num-ber	Endoga-mous	Exoga-mous	Per cent	Num-ber	Endoga-mous	Exoga-mous	Per cent	Num-ber
English	72.9	27.1	100.0	879	73.0	27.0	100.0	465	72.7	27.3	100.0	415
Irish	82.9	17.1	100.0	873	73.0	27.0	100.0	315	88.5	11.5	100.0	557
Scottish	76.2	23.8	100.0	549	69.9	30.1	100.0	246	81.2	18.8	100.0	303
French	96.7	3.3	100.0	1,133	96.9	3.1	100.0	1,119	78.4	21.6	100.0	14
German	72.9	27.1	100.0	237	66.1	33.9	100.0	158	86.6	13.4	100.0	79
Other	72.4	27.6	100.0	85	69.4	30.6	100.0	61	79.8	20.2	100.0	25
Total	82.9	17.1	100.0	3,757	83.4	16.6	100.0	2,364	81.8	18.2	100.0	1,393

SOURCE: Canadian Historical Mobility Project, *1871 Census of Canada*

TABLE 11
Percentage distribution of ethnically endogamous and exogamous marriages by ethnic origin and nativity of husband, Canada, 1971

Ethnic origin of husband	All husbands				Native-born husbands				Foreign-born husbands			
	Endoga-mous	Exoga-mous	Per cent	Num-ber	Endoga-mous	Exoga-mous	Per cent	Num-ber	Endoga-mous	Exoga-mous	Per cent	Num-ber
British	52.2	47.8	100.0	2,059,880	50.0	50.0	100.0	1,701,285	62.2	37.8	100.0	358,580
English	66.9	33.1	100.0	1,247,610	65.6	34.4	100.0	1,017,140	72.5	27.5	100.0	230,465
Irish	28.2	71.8	100.0	371,840	26.9	73.1	100.0	331,255	38.9	61.1	100.0	40,595
Scottish	31.4	68.6	100.0	420,995	27.5	72.5	100.0	339,365	47.6	52.4	100.0	81,625
French	86.2	13.8	100.0	1,217,880	86.5	13.5	100.0	1,187,100	74.7	25.3	100.0	30,785
German	49.2	50.8	100.0	315,570	38.3	61.7	100.0	200,970	68.3	31.7	100.0	114,605
Italian	76.5	23.5	100.0	177,420	30.1	69.9	100.0	35,315	88.0	12.0	100.0	142,105
Dutch	72.2	27.8	100.0	6,230	65.2	34.8	100.0	2,330	76.4	23.6	100.0	3,915
Polish	43.2	56.8	100.0	75,115	24.1	75.9	100.0	38,155	62.8	37.2	100.0	36,965
Scandinavian	21.2	78.8	100.0	92,800	13.6	86.4	100.0	62,275	36.6	63.4	100.0	30,520
Ukrainian	54.0	46.0	100.0	137,245	45.0	55.0	100.0	98,230	76.4	23.6	100.0	39,015
Other	65.4	34.6	100.0	523,355	50.4	49.6	100.0	211,480	75.6	24.4	100.0	311,875
Total	62.7	37.3	100.0	4,605,490	60.4	39.6	100.0	3,537,115	70.4	29.6	100.0	1,068,365

SOURCE: Statistics Canada, 1971 *Census of Canada*, Special Tabulations
NOTE: Total British includes English, Irish, Scottish, and Other British.

nically. The overall level of intermarriage had more than doubled since 1871. The most striking finding is exhibited by native-born husbands of Irish, Scottish, and German origins. The shift represents a major historical change from being over two-thirds endogamous in 1871 to being largely exogamous in 1971. A similar shift also occurred for foreign-born husbands of Irish and Scottish origins. Thus, assimilation of these groups through marriage increased significantly between 1871 and 1971. Several conditions seem likely to have contributed to the shift by the Irish and the Scottish. First, their proportion in the population declined relative to other groups over the century, as demonstrated in Chapter 3 (Table 1), making it more difficult to find wives of their own origin. Second, Canada's increasing ethnic diversity over the twentieth century helped to increase the opportunity for social interaction with women of other origins. Third, women of other origin groups might have seen the Irish and Scottish as desirable groups to marry into, since they were of 'British' origin. As for the Germans, it was somewhat unpopular to be German after the First World War. It is likely that they would therefore choose to blend into Canadian society, and one clear option was assimilation through intermarriage.

Native-born husbands of the other ethnic groups all showed lower levels of ethnic endogamy in 1971 than did the foreign born or total population. The most significant difference is exhibited by Italian native-born husbands: 76.5 per cent of all Italian husbands were endogamous, while only 30.1 per cent of the native born were endogamous. As noted in Chapter 3, Italians are fairly recent twentieth-century immigrants. Their largest influx began after the Second World War and continued into the 1960s. According to the 1971 Census, over half their population was foreign born in 1971. Of the 45.8 per cent native born, three-quarters were second generation, and only one-third were third-plus generation. Hence, it would appear that second generation Italian husbands may have been a classic example of the Hansen thesis, which argues that the second generation often wishes to forget its ethnicity in favour of assimilation. Alternatively, there may have been a shortage of Italian women. In any event, a plausible explanation for the high rates of ethnic intermarriage among native-born Italian husbands could be their high proportion of second generation members.

PROPENSITIES FOR ETHNIC INTERMARRIAGE

The relative sizes and sex ratios of the various groups have a direct influence in determining the limits of possible intermarriage that result from any simple random interaction of individuals in the population (Besanceney 1965; Blau et al. 1982). Propensities are used here as a readily interpreted index that controls for the size and sex ratio of the population from which mates were drawn. The measure compares rates of actual intermarriage to the pattern that could have emerged had all those involved in intramarriages also chosen to outmarry. The index ranges from zero to one. Zero indicates no ethnic intermarriage, and an index of one is indicative of the maximum possible amount of intermarriage.

Table 12 presents intermarriage propensities for native-born, foreign-born, and all husbands of husband-wife families in 1871. The most notable fact is the higher propensity that is revealed for every native-born group, except the French, relative to that exhibited by foreign-born husbands. The pattern suggested for the French is interesting. Native-born husbands have an extremely low propensity for ethnic intermarriage, which is reflective of the high proportion of ethnic endogamy revealed in Table 10. Foreign-born husbands, on the other hand, have the highest propensity for ethnic intermarriage of any of the groups. Again the N is too small to draw firm conclusions. The patterns suggested for all of the other ethnic groups are also worthy of note. Irish foreign-born husbands exhibited the lowest propensity for ethnic intermarriage in 1871, however, there is little variation between the propensities for the remaining groups whether they are foreign or native born.

TABLE 12

Propensities for intermarriage as ratios of 'actual' to 'possible' proportions of ethnic intermarriage, by ethnic origin and nativity of husband, Canada, 1871

Ethnic origin of husband	All husbands		Native-born husbands		Foreign-born husbands	
English	.39	(879)	.40	(465)	.37	(415)
Irish	.33	(873)	.47	(315)	.23	(557)
Scottish	.41	(549)	.48	(246)	.34	(303)
French	.07	(1,133)	.06	(1,119)	.59	(14)
German	.40	(237)	.45	(158)	.30	(79)
Other	.40	(85)	.44	(61)	.33	(25)

SOURCE: Canadian Historical Mobility Project, *1871 Census of Canada*
NOTE: Ns may not add up due to sample weighting.

Table 13 presents the intermarriage propensities for native-born, foreign-born, and all husbands in 1971. Again the most notable fact is the increase in the propensity for ethnic intermarriage for every native-born group, except the French. Significantly higher propensities were exhibited by all Irish and Scottish husbands in 1971 compared to 1871, reflecting the shift from being largely endogamous in the nineteenth century to being largely exogamous by 1971. German native-born husbands also exhibited a significantly higher propensity for ethnic intermarriage in 1971 compared to 1871 and

TABLE 13

Propensities for intermarriage as ratios of 'actual' to 'possible' proportions of ethnic intermarriage, by ethnic origin and nativity of husband, Canada, 1971

Ethnic origin of husband	All husbands		Native-born husbands		Foreign-born husbands	
British[a]	.33	(20,261)	.34	(16,626)	.29	(3,635)
English	.53	–		–		–
Irish	.83	–		–		–
Scottish	.80	–		–		–
French	.25	(12,162)	.24	(11,854)	.61	(308)
German	.66	(3,210)	.76	(2,019)	.45	(1,191)
Italian	.34	(1,754)	.83	(352)	.15	(1,402)
Dutch	.64	(884)	.87	(336)	.39	(548)
Polish	.71	(741)	.87	(379)	.48	(362)
Scandinavian[b]	.82	(893)	.89	(575)	.64	(318)
Ukrainian	.64	(1,401)	.72	(1,028)	.41	(373)
Other	.42	(4,259)	.61	(1,685)	.26	(2,574)

SOURCE: Statistics Canada, *1971 Census of Canada*, 1% Public Use Sample, Family File and Special Tabulations

NOTES: N is given in brackets.

a Includes English, Irish, Scottish, and Other British. The propensity of .33 is calculated from the 1971 Public Use Sample. Propensities for English, Irish, and Scottish are calculated from Special Tabulations. The propensity for ethnic intermarriage for the British (using special tabulations) can be arrived at by adding the three groups together and provides an index of .65. It is significantly higher than the index for the British using the Public Use Sample (.33) because it takes inter- and intramarriage of each group into account, which the PUS does not, since the data are aggregated to begin with. Thus, the use of British in the aggregated form tends to underestimate the propensity for ethnic intermarriage.

b Includes Danish, Swedish, Icelandic, Norwegian, and Scandinavian Not Otherwise Stated

also appear to have made a similar shift in their marriage patterns. Native-born husbands belonging to the French charter group still exhibited relatively low propensities for ethnic intermarriage in 1971, though the increase was substantial, from .06 in 1871 to .24 in 1971.

The patterns for the other ethnic origin groups in 1971, for which there is no comparable 1871 group, are also worthy of note. Italian foreign-born husbands have an extremely low propensity for ethnic intermarriage after controlling for size and sex ratio, while their native-born counterparts have a relatively high propensity for inter-marriage. These results are a reflection of the patterns given in Table 11. Similar comparisons, yielding similar conclusions to those for native- and foreign-born Italians, can be made for the Dutch and the Polish.

In sum, patterns of ethnic intermarriage, as reflected in percent-age distributions of exogamy for native- and foreign-born husbands, revealed greater variation in the twentieth century than in the the nineteenth century among the five major ethnic groups for which comparisons can be made in 1871 and 1971, as one would expect. Similar results are found after controlling for group size and sex ratio. The most striking finding is the historical shift in marriage patterns exhibited by native-born Irish, Scottish, and German hus-bands. Their shift from being overwhelmingly endogamous in 1871 to being overwhelmingly exogamous by 1971 marks them as the most assimilated (through marriage) of the major ethnic groups . While it was not possible to compare data for native-born Scottish and Irish husbands, it is likely that their propensities for ethnic intermarriage would have been even higher in 1971 than they were for all Irish and Scottish husbands combined. Further, both of the charter groups experienced marital assimilation over the century, but were still largely endogamous in 1971. Of the other groups for whom 1971 data only were available, native-born husbands of Ital-ian, Dutch, Polish, and Scandinavian origin all had relatively high propensities for ethnic intermarriage. It is surmised that this pattern reflects their long time residence in Canada. In general, it seems that the salience of ethnicity in the selection of a marriage mate had declined for many of Canada's older immigrant populations by 1971.

PATTERNS OF ETHNIC INTERMARRIAGE FOR SELECTED
ETHNO-RELIGIOUS ORIGINS

This section of the analysis takes Gordon's (1964) position on the multidimensional nature of ethnicity into account so far as the data permit. It examines ethnic intermarriage patterns for selected ethno-religious combinations of husbands. Ethno-religious origins are derived from husband's ethnicity plus his ethnic church, that is, Irish Roman Catholic, Scottish Presbyterian, and the like. The ethnic church was selected in order to maximize the Ns for each ethno-religious origin. Because this definition of cultural origin groups is more precise than when ethnic origin alone is used, and because religion has been shown to reinforce ethnic endogamy, higher rates of ethnic endogamy should be apparent.

Table 14 presents the data for selected ethno-religious origin groups, that is, English Anglicans, Irish Roman Catholics, Scottish Presbyterians, French Roman Catholics, and German Lutherans, for native-born, foreign-born, and all husbands of husband-wife families in 1871. The data reveal patterns similar to those observed in Table 10. As predicted, the percentages of ethnic endogamy are higher for every ethno-religious origin group except for English Anglicans when compared to the percentages in Table 10, where ethnicity was defined in terms of a husband's ethnic or cultural origin alone. The pattern holds for total husbands and native- and foreign-born husbands. The highest relative level of endogamy among native-born husbands was exhibited by Scottish Presbyterians, while German Lutheran husbands showed the greatest relative increase over the data in Table 10 among the foreign born. The effect of making the definition of ethnicity more culturally specific served to dampen the propensity for ethnic intermarriage. Ethno-religious groups clearly represent more culturally cohesive groupings of the population than do the more general ethnic groups commonly used in intermarriage research, at least for the most ethnically connected husbands.

Similar data are presented in Table 15 for native-born, foreign-born, and all husbands of husband-wife families in 1971. Again higher levels of ethnic endogamy are evident for husbands by ethno-religious origins and nativity in 1971 compared to the percentages obtained when only husband's ethnic origin was employed. Of the five comparison groups, German Lutherans showed the greatest relative increase in endogamy as compared to the measure of endogamy among native-born husbands when religion was not a factor. Among foreign-born husbands, Scottish Presbyterians showed the largest relative changes in the measure of endogamy.

The shift from being predominantly endogamous to being predominantly exogamous still holds in 1971 for native-born Irish Catholics and Scottish Presbyterian husbands. The same pattern also holds for foreign-born Irish Catholic husbands, but not for

TABLE 14

Percentage distribution of ethnically endogamous and exogamous marriages by selected ethno-religious origins and nativity of husband, Canada, 1871

Ethno-religious origin of husband	All husbands				Native-born husbands				Foreign-born husbands			
	Endoga-mous	Exoga-mous	Per cent	Num-ber	Endoga-mous	Exoga-mous	Per cent	Num-ber	Endoga-mous	Exoga-mous	Per cent	Num-ber
English												
Anglican	70.5	29.5	100.0	302	69.4	30.6	100.0	111	71.1	28.9	100.0	190
Irish R.												
Catholic	90.9	9.1	100.0	327	79.3	20.7	100.0	71	94.1	5.9	100.0	256
Scottish												
Presbyterian	83.6	16.4	100.0	359	83.0	17.0	100.0	124	84.0	16.0	100.0	236
French R.												
Catholic	97.3	2.7	100.0	1,118	97.5	2.5	100.0	1,108	83.7	16.3	100.0	10
German												
Lutheran	89.8	10.2	100.0	38	73.2	26.8	100.0	9	95.0	5.0	100.0	29
Total	90.1	9.9	100.0	2,144	93.0	7.0	100.0	1,423	84.6	15.4	100.0	721

SOURCE: Canadian Historical Mobility Project, *1871 Census of Canada*
NOTE: Total includes only those groups shown in the table. Other is not shown because the *N*s are too small.

TABLE 15

Percentage distribution of ethnically endogamous and exogamous marriages by selected ethno-religious origins and nativity of husband, Canada, 1971

Ethno-religious origin of husband	All husbands				Native-born husbands				Foreign-born husbands			
	Endoga-mous	Exoga-mous	Per cent	Num-ber	Endoga-mous	Exoga-mous	Per cent	Num-ber	Endoga-mous	Exoga-mous	Per cent	Num-ber
English Anglican	72.9	27.1	100.0	377,295	70.7	29.3	100.0	267,285	78.1	21.9	100.0	110,015
Irish R. Catholic	34.3	65.7	100.0	130,325	32.8	67.2	100.0	116,190	46.4	53.6	100.0	14,135
Scottish Presbyterian	44.9	55.1	100.0	86,110	35.4	64.6	100.0	50,735	58.4	41.6	100.0	35,375
French R. Catholic	89.1	10.9	100.0	1,141,540	89.3	10.7	100.0	1,117,075	82.7	17.3	100.0	24,455
German Lutheran	63.5	36.5	100.0	84,650	50.0	50.0	100.0	39,465	75.3	24.7	100.0	45,195
Italian R. Catholic	79.9	20.1	100.0	166,130	34.4	65.6	100.0	28,170	89.1	10.9	100.0	137,970
Dutch R. Catholic	72.0	28.0	100.0	1,000	67.6	32.7	100.0	185	73.5	26.5	100.0	810
Polish R. Catholic	51.7	48.3	100.0	54,470	30.5	69.5	100.0	23,930	68.3	31.7	100.0	30,530
Scandinavian Lutheran	34.5	65.5	100.0	35,605	22.3	77.7	100.0	17,245	45.9	54.1	100.0	18,365

(continued on next page)

TABLE 15 (continued)

Ethno-religious origin of husband	All husbands				Native-born husbands				Foreign-born husbands			
	Endoga-mous	Exoga-mous	Per cent	Num-ber	Endoga-mous	Exoga-mous	Per cent	Num-ber	Endoga-mous	Exoga-mous	Per cent	Num-ber
Ukrainian Cath./ Orthodox	71.8	28.2	100.0	79,170	65.2	34.8	100.0	47,740	81.9	18.1	100.0	31,430
Other												
R. Catholic	62.7	37.3	100.0	165,190	44.8	55.2	100.0	56,540	72.0	28.0	100.0	108,650
Total	62.7	37.3	100.0	4,605,490	60.4	39.6	100.0	3,537,120	70.4	29.6	100.0	1,068,375

SOURCE: Statistics Canada, *1971 Census of Canada*, Special Tabulations
NOTE: Total is for the total population.

foreign-born Scottish Presbyterians. It seems that Scottish husbands who belong to their ethnic church and were foreign born did not outmarry to the same extent as did their native-born counterparts. It is likely that they were married before their arrival in Canada. Native-born German Lutheran husbands were more endogamous than were German husbands when religion was not a factor (see Table 11), but they were equally exogamous and endogamous (50 per cent) when religion was introduced.

The addition of religious denomination to the definition of ethnicity also affected levels of ethnic intermarriage for husbands of the twentieth century in that being connected to the ethnic church slightly raised their levels of endogamy. This was true for all but Other Roman Catholic husbands.

In general, the use of a more refined or precise definition of ethnicity resulted in higher levels of ethnic endogamy for nearly all ethno-religious origin groups compared to the rates for ethnic origin groups alone in both the nineteenth and twentieth centuries. In addition, the effect of generation was positive in that native-born husbands, in general, had higher rates of marital assimilation than did their foreign-born counterparts. Acknowledgement of the multidimensional nature of ethnicity reveals that the combination of ethnic origin and the dominant ethnic religion had a slight dampening effect on levels of ethnic exogamy for husbands in both centuries because ethno-religious combinations can identify the more culturally cohesive groups within the broader, more ambiguous groupings based on ethnic origin alone.

PATTERNS OF ETHNO-RELIGIOUS INTERMARRIAGE FOR
SELECTED ETHNO-RELIGIOUS ORIGINS

The concept of ethnicity was operationalized to reflect Gordon's (1964) discussion of its multidimensional nature. The notion is adopted in the construction of an index of marital assimilation. The index consists of four different marital types ranging from marriages where husband and wife have different ethnic origins and different religions to the other end of the continuum where their ethnic origins and religious denominations are the same. Thus, the most assimilated are totally exogamous, while the least assimilated are totally endogamous with respect to ethnicity and religion. The rest are either the same ethnically, but different in religion or of the same religion but different ethnically. It has already been demonstrated that, in general, more husbands tend to marry wives of the same ethnic origin than to marry outside their own ethnic group. The pattern is similar for ethno-religious intermarriage. Hence, this section of the analysis focuses on the three pathways to assimilation through marriage for husbands of selected ethno-religious origins who acquired wives outside their own ethno-religious origin. Since research incorporating the multidimensional nature of ethnicity has seldom been conducted, an expected pattern has not been established. Given that, as we have just seen for Canada, outmarriage usually occurs to a greater degree across ethnic lines than across religious lines (Kennedy 1944; Hollingshead 1950; Heer and Hubay 1975), it is expected that, of those husbands who outmarried, the largest proportion would likely have acquired a wife of a different ethnic origin and the same religion, followed by wives who were of the same ethnicity but of a different religion. Following this logic through, it would seem to make sense for the smallest proportion of husbands to have acquired wives of a different ethnic origin and a different religion.

Table 16 reveals the percentage distribution for all husbands of selected ethno-religious origins and the three pathways to assimilation through marriage. As hypothesized, of all the English Anglican, Irish Catholic, and Scottish Presbyterian husbands who married outside their own ethno-religious origin, the largest proportion selected wives of the same religion but of different ethnicity. The smallest proportion married wives of the same ethnic origin but of a different religion. The most interesting finding, however, is the

TABLE 16
Percentage distribution of marital type by ethno-religious origin, Canada, 1871

Ethno-religious origin of husband	Total				
	Diff. ethnic Diff. religion	Same ethnic Diff. religion	Diff. ethnic Same religion	Per cent	Number
English Anglican	33.5	8.6	58.0	100.1	97
Irish R. Catholic	21.4	6.2	72.5	100.1	32
Scottish Presbyterian	22.2	13.0	64.8	100.0	68
French R. Catholic	17.1	–	82.9	100.0	29
German Lutheran	49.6	46.6	3.8	100.0	7
Other Catholic	11.7	–	88.3	100.0	5
Total	26.7	9.5	63.8	100.0	238

SOURCE: Canadian Historical Mobility Project, *1871 Census of Canada*
NOTE: Totals shown are for the groups in the table only.

relatively large proportion of husbands who did not appear to be influenced by either their religion or their ethnicity in their selection of a marriage partner. Just over one-quarter of all husbands are a case in point, along with English Anglicans (33.5 per cent) and German Lutherans (49.6 per cent).

Data for native-born and foreign-born husbands in 1871 are not shown because the Ns for those who outmarried are extremely small,[1] and, under such conditions, the observed patterns might be somewhat unstable. However, a brief comment regarding totals can be made. Data for total native- and foreign-born husbands of the six ethno-religious origins combined reveal the same patterns of mate selection as described above. Again the most interesting finding is the relatively large percentage of husbands who did not appear to be influenced by either their ethnicity or their religion when they selected a marriage mate. Specifically, this was the case for one-third of all foreign-born husbands who chose to marry outside of their own ethno-religious origin and one-fifth of total native-born husbands.

The data in Table 17 present the distribution of marital type by ethno-religious origin and nativity of husbands in 1971. The patterns are rather similar to 1871, with some notable exceptions. Native-born English Anglicans and foreign-born Dutch Catholic husbands who

TABLE 17

Percentage distribution of marital type by ethno-religious origin and nativity of husband, Canada, 1971

Ethno-religious origin of husband	Total				
	Diff. ethnic Diff. religion	Same ethnic Diff. religion	Diff. ethnic Same religion	Per cent	Number
English Anglican	31.3	32.4	36.3	100.0	151,620
Irish R. Catholic	18.6	3.5	77.9	100.0	88,795
Scottish Presbyterian	43.4	10.6	46.0	100.0	53,115
French R. Catholic	21.9	4.2	73.9	100.0	129,480
German Lutheran	39.5	17.5	43.0	100.0	37,485
Italian R. Catholic	22.1	1.8	76.1	100.0	34,075
Dutch R. Catholic	19.8	34.9	45.3	100.0	430
Polish R. Catholic	28.1	1.9	70.0	100.0	26,850
Scandinavian Lutheran	52.2	3.1	44.7	100.0	24,080
Ukrainian Catholic/Ortho.	60.0	15.9	24.0	100.0	26,540
Other R. Catholic	21.7	7.7	70.6	100.0	66,745
Total	25.2	14.0	60.8	100.0	1,997,010

TABLE 17 (continued)

Ethno-religious origin of husband	Diff. ethnic Diff. religion	Same ethnic Diff. religion	Diff. ethnic Same religion	Per cent	Number
		Native born			
English Anglican	30.5	31.5	38.0	100.0	114,285
Irish R. Catholic	17.9	3.4	78.6	100.0	80,885
Scottish Presbyterian	40.6	8.8	50.6	100.0	35,910
French R. Catholic	21.7	4.1	74.1	100.0	124,960
German Lutheran	25.1	6.4	68.5	100.0	4,900
Italian R. Catholic	21.3	0.7	78.0	100.0	18,605
Dutch R. Catholic	42.9	14.3	42.9	100.0	70
Polish R. Catholic	25.5	1.1	73.3	100.0	16,830
Scandinavian Lutheran	48.0	2.5	49.5	100.0	13,745
Ukrainian Catholic/Ortho.	62.7	13.4	23.9	100.0	19,195
Other R. Catholic	18.8	4.3	76.9	100.0	32,605
Total	24.2	12.5	63.2	99.9	1,602,755
		Foreign born			
English Anglican	33.5	35.3	31.2	100.0	37,335
Irish R. Catholic	25.3	4.3	70.4	100.0	7,910
Scottish Presbyterian	49.2	14.5	36.3	100.0	17,215
French R. Catholic	26.5	6.4	67.1	100.0	4,515
German Lutheran	44.8	30.4	24.9	100.0	16,045
Italian R. Catholic	23.1	3.1	73.8	100.0	15,475
Dutch R. Catholic	14.3	38.6	47.1	100.0	350
Polish R. Catholic	32.3	3.3	64.3	100.0	10,020
Scandinavian Lutheran	57.8	4.0	38.3	100.0	10,345
Ukrainian Catholic/Ortho.	53.2	22.5	24.4	100.0	7,345
Other R. Catholic	24.5	10.9	64.6	100.0	34,140
Total	28.9	19.9	51.2	100.0	394,260

SOURCE: Statistics Canada, 1971 Census of Canada, Special Tabulations
NOTES: Totals are for total population. Numbers may not add up due to random rounding.

outmarried are cases in point in that they followed the expected pattern of decreasing percentages from right to left across the assimilation continuum. Of the English Anglican native-born husbands who married outside their ethno-religious origin (exogamous marriages), 38.0 per cent acquired wives of the same religion but of different ethnicity, 31.5 per cent had wives of the same ethnicity but a different religion, and the remaining 30.5 per cent had wives of a completely different ethno-religious origin. Similarly, of the Dutch Roman Catholic foreign-born husbands who married exogamously, 47.1 per cent had wives of a differnt ethnic origin but the same religion, 38.6 per cent had wives of the same ethnic origin but a different religion, and 14.3 per cent had wives of a different ethno-religious origin.

Other husbands deviated from the expected pattern in a different way. The largest proportion of Ukrainian Catholic husbands of both generations, foreign-born Scandinavian Lutherans, Scottish Presbyterians, and German Lutherans who outmarried, for example, acquired wives of a different ethno-religious group. The proportions were largest for native-born Ukrainian Catholics at 62.7 per cent and lowest for Scottish Presbyterians at 49.2 per cent. In other words, a substantial proportion of husbands from these groups did not seem to be influenced by their ethno-religious origin when they married. Size of the group may also have been a contributing factor, especially for husbands who were Dutch Roman Catholics because of their small number.

In sum, only the native-born English Anglicans and foreign-born Dutch Catholics exhibited the expected pattern of decreasing percentages from right to left across the assimilation continuum of the table. Thus, only one of the ethno-religious groups among native-born husbands exhibited the expected pattern, while ten did not. Similarly, only one of the groups among the foreign-born husbands followed the expected pattern, while ten did not.

SUMMARY

The data demonstrate advances in marital assimilation for native-born husbands over the century. Most husbands acquired wives of the same ethnic or ethno-religious origin as themselves. However, significant variation between ethnic and ethno-religious origins between the two time periods was notable. This was especially true for Irish, Scottish, and German husbands who did not fully conform to the pattern exhibited by most groups. By 1971 they had become overwhelmingly exogamous. The same pattern is observed for native-born Irish Catholics and Scottish Presbyterians, but to a slightly less extent. As expected, native-born husbands exhibited higher rates of ethnic exogamy than did foreign-born husbands, since long term residence as reflected by generation has been shown to be positively associated with intermarriage. Exogamy was less in both time periods for ethno-religious origin groups compared to ethnic groups. In general, however, both forms increased over the century, and variations between ethnic groups in patterns of exogamy were more marked in 1971 than in 1871, as expected.

The most significant finding resulting from the analysis of ethno-religious intermarriage seems to be the apparent lack of salience of ethnicity and religion on mate selection for many husbands in 1971. It may be that those who choose to marry outside their ethno-religious origin are individuals who could claim multiple ethnic or cultural origins and/or religions. If this were the case, spouses may be selected from an ethno-religious group included in their repertoire of ethno-religious identities. Intermarriage in the nineteenth century can be characterized, in general terms, as a crossing of ethnic lines. By 1971, however, ethnic-connectedness appeared to have lost its importance to some degree, as indicated by the fact that larger proportions of husbands crossed religious boundaries and/or ethno-religious lines.[2] English Anglicans are a case in point. Only 8.6 per cent crossed religious lines in 1871, while 32.4 per cent did so in 1971. Scottish Presbyterian husbands provide another example: 22.2 per cent crossed both ethnic and religious lines in 1871, but in 1971 the proportion that did so had nearly doubled.

Table 17 summarizes the changes in marital assimilation between 1871 and 1971. The data for ethnic and religious intermarriage support the literature which indicates that individuals will marry outside of their ethnic group more readily than outside of their religious denomination (Kennedy 1944; 1952). The table presents the first data for Canada regarding patterns of ethno-religious intermarriage. The data in Table 18 suggest that assimilation through marriage has increased more than one would expect from looking at the two cultural components separately. It would seem from these data that a single melting pot has been growing since the nineteenth century. It may be argued that this is a result of the definitions of exogamy employed in the table, but the fact remains that by taking more than one cultural component into account, as Gordon (1964) suggested, more blending has occurred than has so far been acknowledged in previous research.

The characteristics of ethnic or cultural groups as a whole, for example, their size, sex ratio, or settlement patterns, could affect an individual member's chances of out-marrying. While data for such group characteristics of ethno-religious origins are unavailable, it is possible to look at the association between selected characteristics for each ethnic group and the individual's propensity for ethnic

TABLE 18

Ethnic, religious, and ethno-religious exogamy of husbands
(as a percentage) by nativity, Canada, 1871 and 1971

Nativity of husband	Ethnic exogamy		Religious exogamy		Ethno-religious exogamy	
	1871	1971	1871	1971	1871	1971
Native born	16.6	25.2	5.5	16.9	19.0	34.7
Foreign born	18.2	19.8	8.0	17.7	21.6	30.3
All husbands	17.1	23.9	6.4	17.1	20.0	33.7

SOURCE: Canadian Historical Mobility Project, *1871 Census of Canada*; Statistics Canada,
1971 Census of Canada, 1 per cent Public Use Sample

intermarriage. Similarly, an individual's characteristics have been
shown to be related to mate selection. The next chapter examines
the relation of both group and individual characteristics to mate
selection and considers the question of who marries whom.

CHAPTER SIX

Group and Individual Factors

'Just as marriage is a two-way street, there is rarely a one-lane avenue to mate selection' (Bernard 1980:90). Individuals do not usually select spouses without regard to the persons around them. Assuming that this is true for both intra- and intermarriages, 'the marital assimilation process must have been at least two-dimensional' (ibid.). The likelihood of marital assimilation, then, depends on both the availability and desirability of potential marriage partners. Over the last five decades, social scientists have attempted to discover the particular social traits of those who married out and those who married within their own group in an effort to isolate the specific characteristics associated with intermarriage. As indicated in Chapter 2, among the many research findings, relationships between intermarriage and an individual's level of education, occupational status, nativity, age, and place of residence were uncovered. This chapter examines the effects of both group and individual characteristics on husbands' propensities for intermarriage in 1871 and 1971. In effect, the analysis tests the applicability of some mid-twentieth-century theories about people who intermarry to the actual occurrences for immigrant populations in Canada, using data from the 1871 and 1971 censuses.

GROUP FACTORS AND PROPENSITIES FOR
ETHNIC INTERMARRIAGE

Ethnic group characteristics, such as the proportion native born, the size of the group, and sex ratio, have been shown to affect an individual's chances to outmarry (Barron 1972; Blau 1977). This section of the analysis presents Spearman's rank order correlation coefficients calculated between the propensities for ethnic intermarriage and various socio-demographic characteristics of ethnic groups. The socio-demographic variables are: percentage urban, percentage of the total population, an index of residential segregation, percentage native born, percentage ethnic religion, sex ratio, percentage illiterate, and percentage in managerial and professional occupations. The Spearman's rank order correlation coefficient (Rho) is a measure of the direction and strength of the relationship and is appropriate where the number of groups compared is small. Its interpretation is similar to Pearson's R, but is usually treated as a rough measure of the degree of association. Rho varies between +1 and –1. The former is indicative of a perfect match of ranks, while –1 indicates that the ranks are exactly opposite. Zero is indicative of no systematic pattern between the ranks.

Spearman's rank order correlation coefficients between husband's propensity for ethnic intermarriage and selected socio-demographic group characteristics in 1871 and 1971 are presented in Table 19. In 1871 the least important factor associated with the propensity for ethnic intermarriage was occupational status. In fact, Rho is almost zero, indicating little or no systematic pattern between the ranks of the two variables. One interpretation is that occupational status in the nineteenth century was more fluid, that is, less rigid, than in the twentieth century; thus, occupations other than those which were

TABLE 19

Spearman's rank order correlation coefficients between propensity for ethnic intermarriage and selected ethnic group characteristics, Canada, 1871 and 1971

Characteristic	1871	1971
Percentage urban	–.614	–.375
Percentage of the population	–.786	–.537
Index of residential segregation	–.214	–.204
Percentage native born	–.386	.104
Percentage ethnic religion	–.300	–.500
Sex ratio	.157	.204
Percentage illiterate	–.386	–.546
Percentage in managerial/professional occ.	–.043	.229

SOURCE: Canadian Historical Mobility Project, *1871 Census of Canada*; Statistics Canada, *1971 Census of Canada*
NOTE: See Appendix B, Table B:1 for indexes of residential segregation used in the calculation of Rho

managerial and professional were considered of equivalent or higher status in the nineteenth century. In addition, only rather small proportions of the groups held these occupations, with larger numbers being farmers (nearly 50 per cent, with craftsmen at about 20 per cent). Alternatively, status differences may not have been that great or important in the nineteenth century.

The association between group size and the propensity for ethnic intermarriage in 1871 was strongest among the socio-demographic factors examined. The coefficient of -.786 indicates a fairly strong negative association with the propensity to intermarry: the larger the size of the ethnic group the lower a husband's propensity for ethnic intermarriage. This result is consistent with mid-twentieth-century findings (Blau 1977; Blau et al. 1982). The French and the Irish are cases in point. They were the two largest ethnic groups in 1871 and, as revealed in Table 12, French and Irish husbands exhibited the lowest propensities for intermarriage.

Studies of the effect of rural/urban residence on intermarriage in the twentieth century produced conflicting findings (Hurd 1942, 1964), so there is no specific expectation. In general, however, urbanity has been expected to increase intermarriage. But the correlation coefficient of -.614 indicates a rather strong negative association between the per cent urban for each ethnic population and the propensity of husbands for ethnic intermarriage in the nineteenth century. That is to say, the less urban an ethnic population, the higher a husband's propensity for ethnic intermarriage. Witness the Germans, who were the least urban of any of the six ethnic groups in the last century, but German husbands exhibited the second highest propensity (.40) for ethnic exogamy in 1871 (Table 12). This finding challenges conventional notions of the influence of urban residence on assimilation.

Indexes of residential segregation[1] were found to be one of the most important factors associated with intermarriage for males in studies of the twentieth century (Hurd 1942). This also appears to have been the case in the nineteenth century, but perhaps to a lesser degree. The data indicate that the higher an ethnic group's index of residential segregation, the lower the propensity of men in the group to marry outside the group. The French, for example, exhibited the highest level of residential segregation in 1871, with an index of 78.5 (Appendix B, Table B:1), and French husbands exhibited the lowest propensity for ethnic exogamy at .07 (Table 12).

An imbalance in the sex ratio was found to favour intermarriage in the twentieth century (Hurd 1929, 1942, 1964; Blau et al. 1982). Findings for the nineteenth century concur, in that a surplus of males was found to be positively associated with a husband's propensity for ethnic outmarriage, albeit weakly associated. The sex ratio for the German origin group was 103.5 in 1871 and the propensity for intermarriage was among the highest for German husbands.

Belonging to the ethnic church is usually associated with ethnic-connectedness. Those belonging to an ethnic church have been shown to be less assimilated than those who report some other religious denomination (Kalbach and Richard 1988a, 1988b). The Spearman's rank order correlation coefficient (–.300) indicates a moderate association between the percentage of a group that is the most ethnically connected in terms of religion and the propensity for ethnic intermarriage of husbands in the group. In other words, the greater the ethnic-connectedness of an ethnic group the lower the propensity of its husbands to intermarry is likely to be. Again the French are the obvious case. They are overwhelmingly Roman Catholic as a group, and the propensity for outmarriage for French husbands is extremely low.

In 1871 the effect of the proportion of native born appears to be moderately strong, but negatively associated with propensities for ethnic intermarriage. This is inconsistent with the expected results based on twentieth-century research. The explanation seems to lie with the effect of the French origin group on the statistic. This group was 99.2 per cent native born in 1871, and husbands exhibited almost no propensity for ethnic intermarriage. When Rho was calculated for five groups (minus the French) it was .075, indicating a positive, but extremely weak, association between the percentage native born of a group and husbands' propensity for intermarriage. These results are congruent with twentieth-century theory.

Immigrant groups with a high proportion of their members achieving high levels of educational attainment are conventionally thought to be more amenable to ethnic intermarriage because they would probably be more liberal in their attitude toward marriage. This theory appears to be true for the nineteenth century. Rho is moderately strong and negative, indicating that the higher an ethnic group's level of illiteracy the lower the propensity of its husbands to outmarry.

In summation, group size and the percentage urban of the group seemed to have the strongest association with the propensities of husbands to ethnically intermarry in the nineteenth century, though both effects were apparently negative. The negative direction of the urban effect was unexpected. High occupational status defined in twentieth-century terms seems to have had little or no association with the propensity of husbands to intermarry in 1871.

It appears that occupational status was somewhat less rigid in 1871 than in the 1900s. Ethnic-connectedness as exemplified by the ethnic church seemed to inhibit intermarriage, although the association appeared to be moderate. Of the remaining group characteristics, residential segregation appears to have had a relatively weak negative effect, sex ratio a positive but even weaker association, and illiteracy and percentage native born moderate negative associations.

Spearman's rank order correlations for 1971 reveal similar results in the direction of the association between intermarriage and percentage urban, group size, index of residential segregation, sex ratio, educational status (as measured by percentage illiterate), and percentage ethnic religion for each ethnic group. The strength of three of these factors, however, seems to be significantly weaker than it was in 1871. The factors are: percentage urban, group size, and residential segregation. In contrast, a group's ethnic-connectedness, level of illiteracy, and sex ratio imbalance appear to be more strongly associated with a husband's propensity to ethnically intermarry in the twentieth century than they were in the nineteenth century.

The index of residential segregation for the French origin group, for example, was the highest overall at 73.5 in 1971, and among French husbands the propensity for ethnic intermarriage was the lowest at .25. In addition, the French origin group also appeared to have the highest level of illiteracy, that is, less than grade five, and again the French exhibited the lowest propensity for intermarriage among husbands in 1971. The association between an ethnic group's occupational status as measured by its proportion in managerial and professional occupations and propensities for husbands to outmarry is revealed by Scandinavians and Germans, each of whom had relatively high levels of occupational status and high propensities among men for ethnic exogamy, .82 and .66, respectively (Table 13).

In summary, the major differences between the two centuries were reflected in occupational status and percentage native born. These seem to have had a relatively weak, but positive, association with propensities for ethnic exogamy exhibited by husbands in 1971. In 1871 the associations were negative, and, in the case of nativity, the association was somewhat stronger, whereas it was much weaker for occupational status. Occupational status as measured in the twentieth century does not appear to have necessarily represented high occupational status in the nineteenth century. In addition, the effect of the generational factor in 1871 seemed to be obscured by the overwhelming proportion of French native-born coupled with their extremely low propensity for ethnic exogamy.

The rank order correlations between a group's ethnic-connected-ness, sex ratio, size, index of residential segregation, and percentage illiteracy with the propensity of its husbands to intermarry were in the expected direction. All were negative in both centuries, except sex ratio, which was positive. The negative correlation of a group's percentage urban and the propensity of its husbands for intermar-riage was unexpected, since it challenges the conventional notions of the influence of urban residence on assimilation.

INDIVIDUAL CHARACTERISTICS AND ETHNO-RELIGIOUS INTERMARRIAGE

Given that the previous section revealed significant associations between group characteristics and intermarriage, one would also expect the characteristics of individuals to affect the likelihood of intermarriage. The effects of literacy, age, nativity, and rural/urban residence on ethno-religious intermarriage in nineteenth- and twen-tieth-century Canada are estimated through minimum logit chi-square regression procedures (Theil 1970; Duncan 1975). This method requires the cross-tabulation of ethno-religious marriages by categories of one or more independent variables. The dependent variable contrasts those husbands who married outside their ethno-religious group with those who married within the group, expressed as the linear transformation of the odds on outmarrying:

$$\ln(N_0 / 1-N_0)$$

where N_0 is the number of respondents who outmarried and $1-N_0$ is the number of individuals who married endogamously. The effects of the independent variables on the likelihood of being ethno-religiously exogamous are expressed as weighted least-squares coefficients.

FINDINGS

Table 20 presents two models each for 1871 and 1971. The first summarizes the main effects and the second shows the interaction effects. The main effects as summarized in Model I reveal that the effect of husband's level of literacy (i.e., illiterate or literate at the time of 1871 and 1971 censuses) is consistent with previous research findings, indicating that individual literacy is associated with inter-marriage (Barron 1972; Jansen 1982). In other words, in both centu-ries being literate increased the likelihood of being exogamous for husbands. Husband's place of residence (i.e., rural/urban) and nativity were also found to have significant effects in both centuries, but in opposite directions. Being native born, for example, had the effect of increasing the likelihood of exogamy for husbands in the nineteenth century, but had the effect of lowering the likelihood of being intermarried at the time of the 1971 Census. Similarly, urban residence increased the likelihood of exogamy for husbands in 1871, but had the effect of lowering the odds on exogamy in 1971. The effects of being urban on the likelihood of intermarriage in 1871 are consistent with Johnson's (1946) research on German outmarriage in 1860 and 1870 in Minnesota, and, in the case of 1971, are consistent with the results of Hurd's (1964) research.

TABLE 20

Effect of age, nativity, residence, and literacy on the likelihood of ethno-religious intermarriage, husbands with spouse present, Canada, 1871 and 1971

Independent variables	1871		1971	
	Model I	Model II	Model I	Model II
Age[1]	.13*	–2.05	–1.15	–.30
	(.14)	(.27)	(.01)	(.04)
Nativity[2]	.30	–.97	–.27	–.23
	(.14)	(.19)	(.01)	(.01)
Rural/urban residence[3]	.45	.47	–.05	.16
	(.18)	(.18)	(.01)	(.01)
Literacy[4]	.94	.30*	.48	1.02
	(.17)	(.17)	(.01)	(.04)
Age X nativity		1.79		–.05
		.22		(.01)
Age X rural/urban residence		–.13*		–.34
		(.24)		(.01)
Age X literacy		1.12		–.56
		(.22)		(.04)
Constant	–2.53	–1.01	–.26	–1.00

SOURCE: Canadian Historical Mobility Project, *1871 Census of Canada*; Statistics Canada, *1971 Census of Canada*, Public Use Sample, Family File
NOTES: ( ) = Standard errors of co-efficients
    * $p > .05$
    [1] Age: 1 = 65+; 0 = 15-24
    [2] Nativity: 1 = native born; 0 = foreign born
    [3] Residence: 1 = urban; 0 = rural
    [4] Literacy: 1 = literate; 0 = illiterate

Finally, considering age, men in the sixty-five and over age group were less likely to have intermarried in 1971 than young men, but age group did not seem to have been a factor influencing intermarriage in the nineteenth century. Note that age in this analysis is represented as a dichotomous variable referring to the two age cohorts, (15–24 and 65+) following Lieberson and Waters, who argue that 'it is not unduly bold to compare age cohorts as a rough way of describing the shifts in out-marriage for groups with a sharp drop-off between the youngest and oldest cohorts' (1985:45).

In summary, when the main effects are considered, being native born, urban resident, and literate had the separate and significant effects of increasing the odds on exogamy for husbands in 1871. These findings are consistent with previous research and a general argument that each contributes to ethnic assimilation (Hurd 1942, 1964; Johnson 1946; Greeley 1971; Alba 1976; Jansen 1982). Only literacy had a similar effect in 1971. Age does not appear to have been a factor in 1871 but appears to indicate decreased odds of intermarriage for husband's over sixty-five years of age in 1971. Contrary to the findings for nineteenth-century husbands, it seems that in 1971 the odds on the likelihood of assimilation through intermarriage were lower among older husbands, urban husbands, and those who were native born. It is striking that the effects of nativity and rural/urban residence on the likelihood of ethno-religious intermarriage are not consistent with other research findings regarding ethnic intermarriage in the twentieth century. The effect of age in 1971, on the other hand, is consistent with the findings of Lieberson and Waters (1985:45), Cohen (1980:118), and Abramson's study of ethnic intermarriage among Catholics (1973:82). Moreover, the effect of residence is consistent with Hurd's findings in his study of ethnic intermarriage in Canada at the time of the 1941 Census, although he dismissed the findings as accidental. It is interesting to note, however, that Abramson found rural Polish Catholics to be more ethnically exogamous than their urban counterparts, although other groups such as the Irish and German Catholics did not conform to these findings (1973:77). A possible explanation of the effect of rural/urban may hinge on differences in the composition of urban areas in so far as the concentration of immigrants is concerned. Perhaps immigrant minority groups were more established or more cohesive in 1971 in urban areas than they were in 1871. The negative effect of being native born on exogamy may be accounted for by the form of the data, that is, native born and foreign born. Separation of the native born into the generational components of second and third-plus generations may produce results consistent with previous findings. It is also possible that highly endogamous French Roman Catholics obscure the generational effect.

The finding that age did not seem to be a factor in ethno-religious exogamy in 1871 also poses a challenge to the generalization that age is generally found to be negatively associated with interethnic and interfaith marriages (Barron 1972:43; 1973:82). In addition, older persons tend to be regarded as more conservative than younger individuals. For these reasons the interaction of age is considered with one of the other independent variables employed in this analysis, both in 1871 and 1971. A second logit regression analysis includes three interaction terms, representing the conditional relationship of age and the other three independent variables. The effects of nativity, rural/urban residence, and literacy, as they are conditioned by age, are presented as Model II in Table 20. Figure 37 presents the results in graphic form.

It can be seen that in 1871 being native born had the effect of increasing the odds on intermarriage among older husbands (coefficient = 1.79). Conversely, it had the effect of lowering the likelihood of outmarriage among husbands who were younger. This is not surprising given the excess of foreign-born males during the nineteenth century and the positive association generally found between generation and intermarriage in the twentieth century (Bossard 1939; Hurd 1942, 1964; Greeley 1971; Alba 1976). Younger foreign-born men had fewer choices of wives of the same ethnicity in Canada, whereas older immigrant men were more likely to have been married before coming to Canada. In addition, level of literacy appears to have had the effect of increasing the odds on intermarriage in 1871, but its effect was most striking among older husbands. The effect of the interaction of rural/urban residence and age on the likelihood of being exogamous was not a significant factor for husbands in 1871.

In 1971 being native born decreased the odds on being exogamous for both age cohorts, as shown in Figure 37, while literacy increased the likelihood of intermarriage among husbands in both age cohorts. The effect, however, was more marked among younger husbands. In contrast to the 1871 period, urban residence raised the odds on being intermarried among young husbands and lowered the odds among their older counterparts. These results indicate that while nativity, literacy, and place of residence exert independent influences on the odds of exogamy, they also tend to be age-specific.

In summary, there appears to be a significant interaction effect between both nativity and literacy by age on the likelihood of assimilation in 1871 and 1971. There also appears to be a significant

FIGURE 37
Effect of husband's nativity and level of literacy on the likelihood of
being intermarried in logged scale by age, Canada, 1871

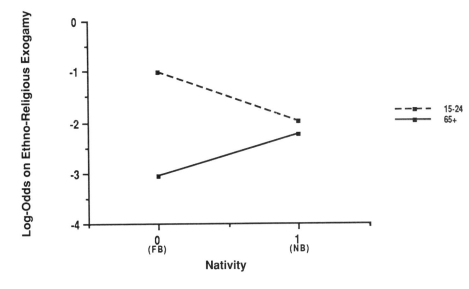

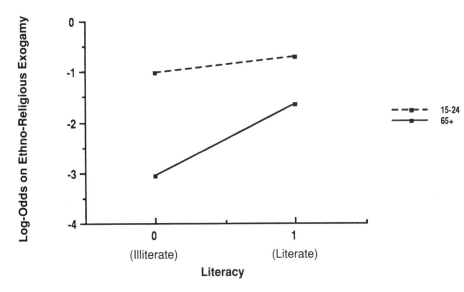

(continued on next page)

FIGURE 37 (continued)
Effect of husband's nativity, level of literacy, and place of residence
on the likelihood of being intermarried in logged scale by age,
Canada, 1971

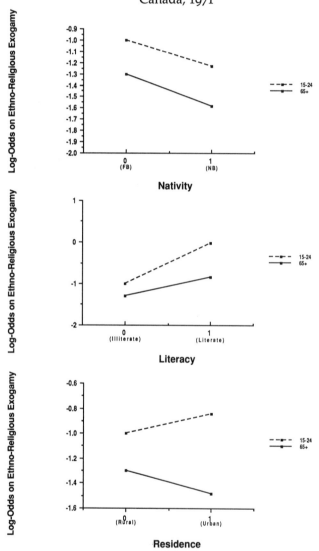

SOURCE: Canadian Historical Mobility Study, *1871 Census of Canada*; Statistics Canada,
1971 Census of Canada, Public Use Sample, Family File
NOTE: FB = Foreign born
    NB = Native born

interaction effect of rural/urban residence and age in 1971, but not in the nineteenth century. Being native born decreased the chances of husbands being assimilated through intermarriage among the fifteen to twenty-four year olds, probably as a result of the limitations on marriage mates within immigrants groups, while being native born increased the likelihood of exogamy among the older husbands in 1871. By the time of the 1971 Census, being native born had the effect of lowering the likelihood of exogamy among husbands in both age cohorts. Being literate increased the likelihood of assimilation through intermarriage in both centuries. This pattern held for both older and younger age cohorts, but was more dramatic among older husbands in the nineteenth century and their younger counterparts of the twentieth century. Literacy has generally been found to be positively associated with marital assimilation, but interactions with age and historical period have not been previously revealed (Greeley 1971; Barron 1972; Jansen 1982).

Urban residence increased the chances of assimilation through exogamy among the fifteen to twenty-four year olds, but was associated with decreased likelihood of assimilation through intermarriage among the older husbands in 1971. The interaction of place of residence and age does not seem to be a factor influencing ethnoreligious exogamy in the nineteenth century.

WHO MARRIED WHOM

Hurd (1929, 1942, 1964) underlined the importance of intermarriage between ethnic minorities and the dominant British and French groups as a means of facilitating assimilation into Canadian society. He was able to show that some groups, like the Northern and Western Europeans, were more likely to intermarry with individuals of British origin than with individuals of other origins. In general, the groups who married least with the British tended to marry with the French and vice versa (Hurd 1942:644). This section examines data from the 1871 and 1971 Censuses to see to what extent husbands married wives of British and French origin and in, that respect, to determine the extent of assimilation. The analysis will also focus on the selection of English wives, since their status is known to be highest relative to other origins (Porter 1965; Berry, Kalin, and Taylor 1977:106–7; Pineo 1987).

Ethnic choices of native- and foreign-born husbands in 1871 are presented in Table 21. Consideration of the six distinctly different ethnic origin groups reveals support for the hypothesis that husbands who married exogamously chose wives of English origin to

TABLE 21

Ethnic origin of husband by ethnic origin of wife by nativity of husband, Canada, 1871

Ethnic origin of husband	Ethnic origin of wife						Total	
	English	Irish	Scottish	French	German	Other	Per cent	Number
NB husbands								
English	39.5	51.5	28.6	7.4	9.6	3.0	100.0	126
Irish	39.5		39.4	6.1	11.9	3.1	100.0	85
Scottish	40.0	41.3		5.4	6.9	6.4	100.0	74
French	31.4	37.5	20.6		5.9	4.6	100.0	35
German	40.9	22.6	10.8	23.5		2.2	100.0	54
Other	42.2	5.5	27.3	13.2	11.9		100.1	19
FB husbands								
English		49.5	36.2	5.3	6.8	2.1	99.9	113
Irish	45.1		39.5	7.3	6.1	2.0	100.0	64
Scottish	42.4	42.2		3.0	10.0	2.5	100.1	57
French	73.8	26.2	–		–	–	100.0	3
German	60.3	16.8	20.3	–		2.6	100.0	11
Other	12.9	68.9	–	11.1	7.2		100.1	6

SOURCE: Canadian Historical Mobility Project, 1871 *Census of Canada*

NOTE: The manner in which the above table should be interpreted is illustrated by reference to the native-born husbands of husband-wife families of German origin. Of all the husbands who married outside their own ethnic origin, i.e., exogamous marriages, 40.9 per cent had wives of English origin, 22.6 per cent had wives of Irish origin, 10.8 per cent had wives of Scottish origin, 23.5 per cent had wives of French origin, and the remaining 2.2 per cent married wives of other origins in 1871.

the greatest extent. Among native-born husbands, for example, larger proportions of German and Others acquired wives of English origin when they married outside their own ethnic group compared to the proportions who selected wives of other ethnic origins. High proportions of Irish, Scottish, and French native-born husbands married wives of English origin, but about the same proportion had also acquired wives of either Irish or Scottish origins. French native-born husbands had a slightly greater tendency to marry Irish wives, probably due to their Catholic affiliations. As far as intermarriage with the French among native-born husbands is concerned, German husbands had the highest percentage of French wives in 1871.

It is also evident that significantly larger proportions of foreign-born husbands married wives of British origins. Furthermore, the proportions are higher than those for native-born husbands. As for the selection of English wives, larger proportions of Irish and German foreign-born husbands married wives of English origin compared to the proportion who married wives of the other origins. Scottish foreign-born husbands followed the same pattern as their native-born counterparts in that 42.4 per cent married English women and 42.2 per cent had Irish wives.

Relatively small proportions of husbands of both generations, except for native-born German husbands, married wives of French origin. No doubt this was due in large part to their high degree of relative concentration in the province of Quebec and underrepresentation elsewhere in Canada in 1871. German husbands who selected French wives may have been German Catholics who wished to marry within their religion. Similar conclusions may be drawn for German husbands who had married wives of Irish origin.

It is recognized that the proportion of husbands who married out of their ethnic group in 1871 was small, and, therefore, caution must be exercised in the interpretation of the data. However, it does appear that the largest proportion of husbands, as expected, acquired wives of English (or British) origin if they married outside their ethnic origin, and that geographical distribution was at least partly responsible for the underrepresentation of French wives attached to husbands who chose to outmarry.

Ethnic choices for native- and foreign-born husbands in 1971 are presented in Table 22. Again it is clear that a significantly larger proportion of husbands of both generations acquired wives of British origins when they married outside their own ethnic group compared to wives of all other ethnic origins. When husbands chose from the pool of non-British wives, those belonging to origins whose ethnic religion is Roman Catholic tended to select wives of origins

TABLE 22

Ethnic origin of husband by ethnic origin of wife by nativity of husband, Canada, 1971

Ethnic origin NB husbands	Ethnic origin of wife									Total	
	British	French	German	Italian	Dutch	Polish	Scandinavian	Ukrainian	Other	Per cent	Number
British		32.8	23.7	3.1	6.4	4.0	10.0	7.8	12.2	100.0	3,360
French	72.7		8.8	2.6	2.1	1.1	2.4	2.9	7.5	100.0	1,606
German	66.7	11.1		0.6	2.3	3.0	4.8	5.5	6.1	100.0	1,254
Italian	53.7	26.6	2.3		0.8	1.9	2.3	5.4	6.9	100.0	259
Dutch	67.6	6.9	12.1	0.4		1.2	3.6	3.2	4.9	100.0	247
Polish	44.5	11.4	9.0	0.3	3.1		4.1	19.3	8.3	100.0	290
Scandinavian	59.2	6.0	13.6	1.8	2.5	3.1		6.9	6.9	100.0	448
Ukrainian	46.9	10.8	11.3	2.0	2.0	9.6	6.6		10.7	100.0	591
Other	57.6	16.1	10.0	1.5	2.1	2.9	6.0	3.9		100.0	722

Ethnic origin FB husbands	Ethnic origin of wife									Total	
	British	French	German	Italian	Dutch	Polish	Scandinavian	Ukrainian	Other	Per cent	Number
British		26.5	22.9	5.1	5.5	3.6	9.1	7.6	19.8	100.0	475
French	56.1		18.2	6.1	3.0	–	3.0	–	13.6	100.0	66
German	55.0	9.5		1.9	4.4	2.5	5.2	4.9	16.6	100.0	367
Italian	43.7	23.4	7.2		3.0	1.2	–	5.4	16.2	100.0	167
Dutch	65.1	4.1	14.0	0.6		0.6	2.9	2.3	10.5	100.0	172
Polish	38.1	9.0	11.2	2.2	0.7		1.5	20.9	16.4	100.0	134
Scandinavian	66.9	6.9	8.6	0.6	1.7	2.3		1.7	11.4	100.0	175
Ukrainian	33.7	7.0	14.0	2.3	1.2	27.9	1.2		12.8	100.0	86
Other	43.9	16.2	20.7	3.2	3.4	4.9	2.1	5.7		100.0	474

SOURCE: Statistics Canada, 1 per cent Public Use Sample, Family File, *1971 Census of Canada*

NOTE: The manner in which the above table should be interpreted can be illustrated with reference to the native-born husbands of husband-wife families of Dutch origin. Of all the husbands who married outside their own ethnic origin, i.e., exogamous marriages, 67.6 per cent had wives of British origins, 6.9 per cent had wives of French origin, 12.1 per cent had wives of German origin, 0.4 per cent had wives of Italian origin, 1.2 per cent had wives of Polish origin, 3.6 per cent had wives of Scandinavian origin, 3.2 per cent had wives of Ukrainian origin, and the remaining 4.9 per cent married wives of Other origins in 1971.

that were also ethnically connected to the Roman Catholic church, that is, French, Dutch, and German. High proportions of other husbands, such as those of Polish origin, also selected wives from ethnic groups that were culturally similar (e.g., Ukrainians).

In view of the fact that significantly larger proportions of husbands chose British wives if they outmarried compared to wives of other origins, it would be interesting to see what the pattern would be if the British were separated into English, Irish, and Scottish, since such data have not been examined in previous research. The expectation is that the British components would marry each other to the greatest extent and that significantly larger proportions of husbands of other origins would have chosen wives from the English origin group. Data for husbands by nativity were unavailable, but data for all husbands combined are presented in Table 23. As hypothesized, a significantly larger proportion of husbands acquired wives of English origin, if they married outside their ethnic origin, than from any other group. The largest proportions of English husbands chose wives of Scottish origin followed by Other and Irish wives. Similarly, the largest proportion of Irish husbands who outmarried chose wives of English and Scottish origins, and nearly 50 per cent of Scottish husbands acquired wives of English origin, while nearly 19 per cent married wives of Irish origin.

The relative sizes of the ethnic populations from which wives were selected would lead one to expect that a large percentage of exogamous marriages would be with persons of English and French origins, all other things being equal, including geographical distribution. In the case of English native-born husbands, however, who selected wives from the non-English pool in 1871, only 7 per cent married wives of French origin. In other words, French wives appear to have been significantly underrepresented considering the fact that they comprised 58.2 per cent of all non-English wives in 1871. In 1971 similar conclusions are reached, but French wives were underrepresented to a lesser degree. French wives, in this case, made up 38 per cent of non-English wives, but only 15 per cent of English native-born husbands selected them as spouses. It is likely that this underrepresentation is related to the high degree of relative concentration of the French in the province of Quebec in 1871 and in Quebec and New Brunswick in 1971, but it represents the strength of the cultural and linguistic barriers characteristic of French-English relations in Canada. In addition, there was a legacy of prejudice and mistrust dividing the 'two solitudes' of Canada.

In summation, it appears that larger proportions of husbands who married outside their own ethnic origin in both centuries acquired

TABLE 23

Percentage distribution of ethnic origin of husband by ethnic origin of wife, for the total population, Canada, 1971

Ethnic origin of husband	Ethnic origin of wife							Total	
	English	Irish	Scottish	Other Br. Is.	French	German	Other	Per cent	Number
English		22.4	26.8	1.1	15.6	11.3	22.7	99.9	412,795
Irish	44.2		19.5	0.9	13.9	7.8	13.7	100.0	266,855
Scottish	49.2	18.7		1.1	9.1	7.5	14.3	100.0	288,715
Other British Isles	40.6	13.9	17.3		6.0	6.6	15.6	100.0	17,005
French	42.7	17.8	11.8	0.4		8.3	19.4	100.4	168,335
German	37.5	13.2	13.4	0.7	10.7		24.5	100.0	160,345
Other	40.5	13.1	14.3	0.9	16.1	15.0		99.9	295,025

SOURCE: Statistics Canada, 1971 Census of Canada, Special Tabulations
NOTE: Other British Isles includes Welsh. For the interpretation of this table see note for Table 22

wives of English origin compared to the proportions who had wives of other origins. The same is generally true for those who acquired British wives. In the case of British wives it may also have been due to their greater numbers relative to those of other ethnic origins. Extending Hurd's conclusions, then, assimilation through intermarriage with the English progressed over the century. Intermarriage with the French also seems to have progressed, since French wives were not as underrepresented in 1971 as they were in 1871.

CHAPTER SEVEN

Conclusion

Classical assimilation theory indicates that some assimilation of ethnic and cultural groups is expected and, indeed, is inevitable in any society. This research deals specifically with the question of marital assimilation. It has delineated the general trends of ethnic and ethno-religious intermarriage between 1871 and 1971, as well as the trends for the English, Irish, Scottish, French, and Germans. In addition, it has determined the effects of husband's level of literacy, nativity, age, and place of residence on the odds of marrying outside his ethno-religious origin and the effect of an ethnic group's socio-demographic characteristics on the propensity for husbands to marry exogamously. The variables included in the latter analysis are group size, sex ratio, ethnic-connectedness (i.e., religion), percentage urban, occupational status, educational attainment, indexes of residential segregation, and percentage native born. Furthermore, this research has determined the progress of assimilation from the standpoint of intermarriage with the British (or English) and the French. This chapter summarizes the findings of this study and discusses the implications of marital assimilation for Canadian society.

This research has demonstrated the value of intermarriage as an index and a measure of assimilation. It has been widely used by Canadian and American social scientists in their quest to determine the patterns, correlates, and relevance of intermarriage for immigrant assimilation in the twentieth century. Canadian research demonstrated increasing trends of religious and ethnic intermarriage in Canada between 1921 and 1971 (Hurd 1929, 1942, 1964; Kalbach 1975, 1983; Heer and Hubay 1975). Evidence from twentieth-century research indicates that the notion of the 'triple melting pot' is not applicable to the Canadian situation, but rather that Canada seemed to have a melting pot of her own, different from that envisioned in the United States. Intermarriage rates of the twentieth century showed considerable variation between ethnic groups, a propensity for individuals to select marriage partners from the numerically dominant groups (i.e., the British and French), and/or a preference for spouses of cultural backgrounds similar to their own. Similar to the United States, however, ethnic intermarriage was shown to occur more frequently than religious exogamy.

This study reports the first data on intermarriage in nineteenth-century Canada. What is known about nineteenth-century patterns and correlates comes from American data, but overall very few studies have been undertaken. In general, this research provides initial support for Gordon's theory of the importance of structural assimilation as a stepping stone to intermarriage.

The data used in this research are taken from the 1871 and 1971 censuses. Small numbers of nineteenth-century outmarriers precluded, in some cases, the examination of such factors as provincial differences and the use of the multidimensional definition of ethnicity. Nevertheless, this analysis marks the first time Canadian data has been available in a form that makes possible an analysis of nineteenth-century intermarriage, and, hence, enables a comparison with twentieth-century findings. Moreover, it appears to be the only analysis to date that examines the ethno-religious dimension of intermarriage in the spirit of Gordon's (1964) theoretical framework.

Levels of ethnic intermarriage were lower in nineteenth century Canada than in the twentieth century (Hurd 1929, 1942, 1964; Kalbach 1975, 1983). But given that they were found to be on the increase between 1921 and 1971, this finding conforms to the expectation for patterns before the turn of the century. The nineteenth-century results confirm that assimilation though marriage was occurring in Canada as early as 1871. They also confirm the importance of intermarriage in the assimilation of ethnic groups in Canadian society. The importance of intermarriage for assimilation is indicated by the relatively high proportions of 1871 husbands who, if they married outside their own ethnic group, had acquired wives of British (English) and French origins, although the proportions doing so were lower in the nineteenth century than in 1971. This probably reflects their shorter length of residence in Canada at the time of the 1871 census compared to a hundred years later.

The significance of intermarriage as an index and a method of assimilation is further underlined by the major historical shift exhibited by native- and foreign-born Irish and Scottish, as well as native-born German husbands, from being overwhelmingly endo-gamous in 1871 to being largely exogamous in 1971. The explanation of this phenomenon includes the declining proportions of the Irish and Scottish relative to other groups in Canada as the twentieth century progressed, making it more difficult for husbands of these groups to find wives of the same ethnic origin. Moreover, being part of the 'British' probably enhanced their desirability as marriage mates. Germans, on the other hand, were no doubt influenced by the disdain they had to endure during the two great world wars. It is likely that they were more motivated than other groups to assim-ilate quickly or to blend into Canadian society in order to avoid the stigma attached to being German.

As hypothesized, differentials in propensities to intermarry eth-nically were found. These differences between husbands of the six ethnic groups were slight in 1871, but had increased dramatically by 1971. In addition, the propensities for ethnic exogamy exhibited by French and German native-born husbands had almost doubled by 1971. Data were unavailable for a direct comparison of 1871 and 1971 husbands of Irish and Scottish origins by nativity, but it is likely that their propensities would show significant increases over the hun-dred-year period given the results for all husbands of these groups: propensities for total Irish and Scottish husbands doubled between 1871 and 1971. In view of these results, it can be seen that the aggregation of the British components severely underestimates the amount of intermarriage in Canadian society. Similarly, the lumping together of the Scandinavians or any other similar cultural groups also leads to significant underestimation of the progress of assimi-lation, from the standpoint of intermarriage, in any time period.

French husbands were more likely to intermarry in 1971 than in 1871. Their propensity for ethnic exogamy doubled for native-born husbands, but remained about the same at relatively high levels for husbands who were foreign born. The fact that French foreign-born husbands exhibited a high propensity for intermarriage in 1971 lends credence to the patterns exhibited by a much smaller number of their 1871 foreign-born counterparts. Lower levels of assimilation through marriage are not unexpected for the French for several reasons, both demographic and cultural. They were large in number relative to other groups in both time periods and were highly concentrated in the Province of Quebec, and as such, are a good example of the effect of propinquity and group size on levels of marital assimilation. There are, in addition, the social and political forces in favour of linguistic and cultural maintenance of Quebec society.

Considering the multidimensional nature of ethnicity in the analysis produced some interesting results. It was shown that in the case of ethnicity, as expected, the overwhelming choice of husbands was to select a spouse of the same ethno-religious origin. Husbands who married outside their ethno-religious group did not conform to the hypothesized pattern. Among husbands who outmarried, the most assimilated were considered those to have acquired a wife of a different ethnicity and a different religion. Husbands who took wives of a different ethnic or cultural origin, but the same religion, were considered the least assimilated. In the middle of the continuum were husbands who married wives of the same ethnicity as their own but of a different religion. It was expected that the proportions of husbands who outmarried in 1871 and 1971 would increase along the continuum from most to least assimilated.

The results of this analysis are striking. Of husbands who outmarried in 1971 the largest proportion selected wives of a different ethnicity, but stayed within their religious affiliation. But the second largest proportion of husbands in nearly every case married outside their ethno-religious origin group altogether. It would appear that a significant proportion of exogamous husbands were not influenced by their ethno-religious connection in their choice of a marriage partner in 1971. It may be that if one were motivated to assimilate strongly enough to cross religious lines in search of a mate, crossing of ethnic lines would be of no consequence. Hence, there would be no innate 'left to right' continuum. Perhaps the ethnic group boundary is the inevitable boundary that must be crossed in order to become Canadianized or Anglo-Saxonized. Similar results were found for native-born, foreign-born, and all husbands in 1871, but small Ns precluded the presentation of data for the latter two categories. However, the fact that the patterns of mate selection were nearly identical in both centuries underlines the probability that the patterns observed for husbands in 1871 were indicative of an historic trend lasting throughout the century. These results lend support to the notion that the triple melting pot is not applicable to Canadian society (Kalbach 1975, 1983). Instead, the evidence suggests that Canada has had a single melting pot since 1871. In any case, there is no doubt that Canada's immigrants have been gradually blending through marriage to a much greater extent than previously thought.

Bernard (1980) examined the effects of both group and individual characteristics on patterns of intermarriage in Wisconsin. He argued that group characteristics appeared to be the most useful for understanding patterns of ethnic intermarriage, especially for Eastern

Europeans. While it was not possible to replicate his analysis with the available Canadian data, it was possible to examine the effect of ethnic group and individual characteristics on propensities for ethnic intermarriage. The analysis shows that both group character-istics and husbands' individual characteristics were significant determinants of the patterns observed in nineteenth- and twen-tieth-century Canada.

For the most part, the findings of this research regarding the effects of a group's socio-demographic factors were in concert with twentieth-century findings, but some important differences were also found. It should be recognized, however, that inferences about the influences of some of the factors in this analysis, for example, occupational status and educational attainment, comes mainly from findings regarding individual characteristics. In any case, it was argued that if an ethnic group is perceived as being of low status it is likely that husbands belonging to that group would be considered less desirable as marriage partners by women from other ethnic groups. In general, there were slight variations in the strength of the associations found between intermarriage and group characteristics for the two time periods, and their rank order in terms of that strength did not coincide in both centuries. Group size, for example, exhibited a slightly stronger negative association between a hus-band's propensity to marry outside his ethnic group in 1871 com-pared to 1971 and showed the strongest association of any factor with the propensity to outmarry in the nineteenth century. Group size ranked second among the various factors in 1971. Similarly, the extent of a group's urban residence exerted the same effect in both centuries, but ranked second in strength in 1871 and fourth in 1971.

Two major exceptions to twentieth-century findings stand out, namely, the effects of a group's percentage native born and its proportion engaged in managerial and professional occupations. Virtually every study has found a positive relationship between nativity and levels of ethnic exogamy (Hurd 1929, 1942, 1964; Kennedy 1944, 1952; Hollingshead 1950; Kalbach 1975, 1983). More-over, twentieth-century research indicates that the majority of the foreign born were already married when they arrived in Canada (Kalbach 1970). Thus, studies seeking to determine propensities to intermarry in the twentieth century tend to concentrate on native-born husbands (Kalbach 1975; 1983). The findings of this research suggest that one must also look at patterns for foreign-born hus-bands in order to accurately ascertain propensities for intermarriage in nineteenth century Canada. This makes sense because immigra-tion tends to favour males, especially in the nineteenth century.

Moreover, transportation to the new world was not as accessible or as cheap in the nineteenth century as it was in the mid-twentieth century. One confounding factor, however, was the French population, with its extremely high proportion of native born coupled with an almost non-existent propensity to intermarry. The exclusion of this group from the rank order correlation analysis for 1871 changed the relation between generation and the propensity to outmarry ethnically to a positive value, but weak association. Nonetheless, it would appear that an examination of patterns of intermarriage for foreign-born husbands is warranted in order to obtain a more accurate picture of nineteenth-century intermarriage.

The second major exception to twentieth-century findings deals with occupational status as reflected by the proportion of the ethnic group engaged in managerial and professional occupations. A weak but positive association between high occupational status and the propensity to marry exogamously was exhibited in 1971. This agrees with findings from twentieth century research. In 1871, however, the relationship was extremely weak and negative. This appears to reflect the fact that the twentieth-century definition of high occupational status did not apply in the nineteenth century and may also be indicative of the more fluid or less rigid nature of occupational status at that time.

It can be concluded that neither a group's percentage native born nor its status as measured by the percentage working in managerial and professional occupations are helpful explanatory factors of propensities for ethnic intermarriage in nineteenth-century Canada. On the other hand, this research demonstrates that there were negative associations between the propensity of a husband to marry outside his ethnic group and the group's level of literacy, level of residential segregation, level of ethnic-connectedness (as measured by the percentage belonging to the ethnic church), size, and percentage urban. In addition, the sex ratio of the group had a positive and significant association with intermarriage.

Following research on ethnic and religious intermarriage, statistical models of the relationship between selected individual characteristics and ethno-religious intermarriage were tested. An analysis of individual characteristics was undertaken by means of logit regression. When only the main effects of the model were considered, being native born, urban resident, and literate had the separate and significant effect of increasing the odds on ethno-religious exogamy for husbands in 1871. Only literacy had a similar effect in 1971. Age does not appear to have been a factor in 1871, but appears to indicate decreased odds of ethno-religious intermarriage for husband's sixty-five years of age and over in 1971. These findings are consistent with previous research dealing with ethnic and religious intermarriage (Hurd 1942, 1964; Johnson 1946; Greeley 1971; Alba 1976; Jansen 1982). The 1871–1971 differences suggest that although assimilation through intermarriage was evident in both centuries, the processes through which it was attained differed considerably. It is particularly striking that the effects of nativity and rural/urban residence on the likelihood of ethno-religious exogamy are not consistent with other research findings. The effect of age in 1971, however, is consistent with the literature (Abramson 1973; Cohen 1980; Lieberson and Waters 1985), though not in 1871, and the effect of rural/urban residence is consistent with Hurd's (1964) findings in 1941.

The results of the second logit regression analysis showing the effects of husband's nativity, literacy, and rural/urban residence as they are conditioned by age showed that while each exerted independent influences on the odds of exogamy, they also tended to be age-specific. There were, for example, significant interaction effects between both nativity and literacy by age on the likelihood of assimilation in 1871 and 1971. There also appears to be a significant interaction effect of rural/urban residence and age in 1971, though not in the nineteenth century. Being native born decreased the chances of husbands being assimilated through ethno-religious intermarriage among the fifteen to twenty-four year olds (probably as a result of the limitations on marriage mates within immigrant groups), but increased the likelihood of ethno-religious exogamy among older husbands in 1871. By the time of the 1971 Census, being native born had the effects of lowering the likelihood of exogamy among husbands in both age cohorts. Being literate increased the likelihood of assimilation through intermarriage in both centuries. This pattern held for both older and younger age cohorts, but was more dramatic among older husbands in the nineteenth century and their younger counterparts in the twentieth century. Literacy has generally been found to be positively associated with marital assimilation, but interactions with age and historical period have not previously been revealed.

Urban residence increased the chances of assimilation through ethno-religious exogamy among the fifteen to twenty-four year olds, but decreased the likelihood of assimilation through intermarriage among the older husbands in 1971. The interaction of place of residence and age does not seem to have been a factor influencing ethno-religious exogamy in the nineteenth century.

CONCLUSIONS

The results of this analysis indicate that ethnic and ethno-religious intermarriage in Canada doubled during the hundred-year period between 1871 and 1971. Assimilation with the British and French from the standpoint of intermarriage also showed increases over the century. The two charter groups were, in turn, affected by immigrant groups. The British and French showed evidence of marital assimilation over the century, but, as the numerically and/or culturally dominant groups, their levels of intermarriage were among the lowest. This research has demonstrated the utility of examining data for the individual components of the British origin group. English husbands followed a pattern similar to that for the British as a whole, but major historical changes were exhibited by Scottish and Irish husbands. Similar patterns were exhibited by German husbands. When intermarrying, larger proportions of husbands from all ethnic groups tended to select wives from the British origin groups, especially from the English, in both centuries. Likewise, when English, Irish, and Scottish husbands outmarried, they tended to choose wives from among the other British origin groups.

These patterns of intermarriage reveal something about the social distance between groups in 1871 and 1971. Had there not been social and cultural boundaries between groups one might assume that the patterns observed would have been dependent only upon the size of the groups. It has been shown that husbands who married outside their own group showed strong preferences for wives of specific origins in both time periods and that these preferences did not diminish over time.

One of the results of increasing ethnic intermarriage is larger proportions of the population who are also of mixed ethnic origins. As Lieberson and Waters suggest, 'this means that the behaviour of persons of mixed ancestry are of considerable relevance for understanding current and future trends' (1985:43). In terms of increases in ethnic intermarriage it does not necessarily follow that a decline in the salience of ethnicity for the children of these intermarriers has also occurred because, if they marry, it is possible that they will show 'patterns of ethnic affinity in their own marriage behaviour' (ibid.: 44). In fact, Lieberson and Waters demonstrate that this was the case in the United States. As they suggest, new questions can now be asked about intermarriage, questions that differ from the type that have been addressed in this analysis. However, Canadian data are not yet available in a form that would facilitate such an analysis. While multiple origins are provided in the 1981 Public Use

Sample, the categories are too general to replicate Lieberson and Waters's U.S. analysis.[1] Nevertheless, it follows from the present analysis that larger proportions of the population will not only be of mixed ancestry, but also that increasing proportions will be of mixed ethno-religious ancestry.

Ethnicity is a multidimensional phenomenon which especially involves religion (Gordon 1964). Combinations of ethno-religious boundaries more closely identify meaningful cultural groups and these combinations are reflected in other behavioural characteristics (Kalbach and Richard 1988). Failure to take this multidimensionality into account may be one reason that results in previous research suggest that ethnic origin has diminished in salience (see Boyd et al. 1985). In view of the emphasis placed on the impact ethnicity and religion have on one another, this research has shown that it is more enlightening to examine patterns of intermarriage which include both. The most significant result is the striking proportion of husbands for whom neither ethnicity nor religion appeared to influence mate selection in a restrictive sense. Following Lieberson's and Waters's argument, this does not necessarily mean that the salience of their ethnic-connectedness has diminished. It may be that these husbands are themselves offspring of earlier ethno-religious inter-marriers, expressing patterns of ethno-religious affinity in their own marriage behaviour. It may also be that other ethnic or ethno-religious groups may be seen to be more important than their own ethnic or ethno-religious origin.

In summary, this research has gone beyond current knowledge of patterns of intermarriage and correlates through the addition of new research findings arising from the use of data that were previously unavailable to researchers, namely the 1871 Census of Canada. It also marks the first time that a detailed comparative analysis of ethno-religious intermarriage has been undertaken.

Increasing ethnic and ethno-religious intermarriage is evident between 1871 and 1971. Irish, Scottish, and German husbands assimilated to the greatest extent through marriage during the century. Husbands belonging to the two charter groups also experienced effects of marital assimilation, but were still largely endogamous in 1971. English wives were acquired most frequently in both the nineteenth and twentieth centuries, followed by their other British counterparts. The consistent attractiveness of the English (British) as marriage partners is reflective of the continuation of status differences between Canada's ethnic or cultural groups.

For the most part, twentieth-century theories were applicable to the nineteenth century. Size of the group, sex ratio, and educational status were all associated with higher levels of ethnic exogamy. Major exceptions were the percentage native born and occupational status. It is likely, however, that a group's percentage native born would also have conformed to expectations if the population in 1871 had been more heterogeneous with respect to nativity and indexes of relative concentration. The presence of the French, with their high levels of concentration in Quebec, their high proportion of native born, their high level of ethnic-connectedness, and their extremely low propensity to intermarry, appear to have weighted the results such that it either reduced the significance of group characteristics for intermarriage when they were removed from the calculations or reversed the expected result. This was not the case for occupational status, however. The historical reality of the nineteenth century was not one of necessarily attributing high status to husbands engaged in professional and managerial occupations only. Occupational status appears to have been less rigid in the nineteenth century than it was in the twentieth century.

Some of the effects of a husband's characteristics on the likelihood of ethno-religious exogamy deviated from the findings expected based on the results of previous work on ethnic intermarriage. A case in point is the effect of generation as conditioned by age in both time periods. A husband's place of residence (rural/urban) conditioned by age exhibited no effect on the odds of being ethno-religiously intermarried in 1871, but was a factor in 1971. This would seem to support the notion that there is merit in the utilization of Gordon's recommendation for using a more complete definition of ethnicity.

This research has demonstrated that the use of a single concept, that is, ethnic origin or religion, to delineate patterns and rates of intermarriage in Canada tends to result in an underestimation of the amount of martial assimilation that has taken place. Moreover, this work has also demonstrated that the aggregation of similar ethnic or cultural groups, that is, British and Scandinavian, also results in an underestimation of the phenomenon. These findings indicate the importance of preserving distinct ethnic origin groups as well as the importance and significance of considering both religion and ethnicity when conducting research on ethnic groups in Canada.

This book documents patterns, rates, and correlates of marital assimilation for husbands in nineteenth- and twentieth-century Canada and indicates that the blending of Europeans in Canadian society has progressed differentially since 1871. Excluding the French, the groups that have been resident the longest (e.g., Irish) and those of the smallest size (e.g., Scandinavians) have assimilated the most. The evidence suggests that marital assimilation is likely to continue into the future, but there are obvious differences, both between and within ethno-religious groups, that are associated with differences in potential for marital assimilation in Canadian society. Whether the experiences of the European ethno-religious origin groups will have some validity for understanding marital assimilation patterns exhibited by the more visible minorities that have dominated the migration stream of the late 1970s and 1980s remains to be seen. This could be a subject for future research.

While ethno-religious intermarriage has progressed in Canadian society, individuals are still strongly affected by their ethno-cultural origins in their choice of a marriage partner. It is not known whether the sons and daughters of husbands and wives in Canada who chose marriage as a pathway to assimilation will continue to be influenced by either of their parents' ethno-cultural identities. Lieberson and Waters (1985) have shown that in the United States this is the case for some individuals of mixed ancestry. There is no reason, at the moment, to expect that it would be otherwise for those of mixed ethno-religious ancestry in Canada. This could also be a subject for future research.

Ethnic origin data from the census are indicative of an individual's cultural roots. Such data do not shed light on a person's current ethnic identity. Survey research, however, could be undertaken to ascertain current ethnic identity and other social psychological determinants and correlates of intermarriage, such as the strength of an individual's identity or attitudes toward other ethnic origin groups. These areas of interest are also subjects for future research and are currently under investigation.

Appendices

Variables

The 1871 and 1971 censuses provide data for six and nine ethnic origin groups, respectively, and these furnish the basis for distinguishing between ethnic endogamy and ethnic exogamy in this analysis. Similarly, data for religious denominations are used to determine religious intra- and intermarriage. These two variables are used in combination to derive an index of marital assimilation. The analysis focuses on only the four provinces in the Dominion in 1871 and all of the provinces for which data are provided in the 1971 Public Use Sample.[1] The decision to consider all available provincial data for 1971, rather than the four provinces that comprised Canada in 1871, was taken in order to generalize to the entire 'Canadian' population in each century and to maximize the Ns for each ethnic group.

The specific variables employed in this analysis and their definitions are as follows, as given in the *Dictionary of the 1971 Census Terms* (Statistics Canada 1972), *Historical Statistics of Canada* (Urquhart and Buckley 1965; Leacy 1983), the 1871 Census volumes, and the Canadian Historical Mobility Project:

1 Ethnic origin: In 1871 ethnic origin referred to racial origin and was a mixture of biological, cultural, and geographic attributes. In 1971 it referred to the ethnic or cultural background traced through the father's side.

2 Religion: refers to the specific religious body, denomination, sect, or community of which the individual is a member or which the person adheres to or favours in both 1871 and 1971. The specific question asked in 1971 was, 'What is your religion?'

3 Nativity: refers to whether a person was born in or outside Canada, i.e.,

native or foreign born. The word generation is used as a synonym for nativity, but is also used to refer to first, second, and third-plus generations.

4 Age: refers to the respondent's actual age in years at the time of the census. Two age cohorts are utilized, those 15 to 24 and those 65 years of age and over, i.e., the youngest and the oldest.[2]

5 Sex: refers to the gender of the respondent.

6 Marital status: refers to the conjugal status of a person. The 1871 Census did not report separated or divorced. The 1971 Census reports both.

7 Occupation: refers to those who were gainfully employed (1871 Census) or in the labour force (1971 Census) and the work they were doing or looking for at the time of the census. In 1971 an individual's occupation was determined by his/her description of the most important duties and job title.

8 Literacy: In order to determine the literacy of the population in 1871, data were collected on whether a person could read or write. Information was also collected on whether a person was attending school. The basic literacy question, however, has not been asked since the early twentieth century, when literacy was no longer deemed a problem in Canadian society. Therefore, the census variable used to measure literacy in 1971 is level of schooling, which refers to the highest grade or year of elementary school, secondary school, or university attended. For the purpose of this analysis illiteracy is measured by the proportion of those with less than a grade five level of completed schooling in 1971. While this may overestimate the degree of illiteracy, it was selected on the basis of the researcher's teaching experience at the elementary level. Reading skills are taught at the primary level, that is, grades one through four. Hence, anyone who has not completed the primary grades may not be able to read and write. This definition seems to fall in line with the current UN (1965) definition of literacy, which is the ability to read and write. The inability to do both makes a person illiterate. While it is recognized that there is much debate on the subject of illiteracy and its definition, and that the definition chosen for 1971 is not the same as that for 1871, the two are sufficiently comparable to allow an analysis of the differences in educational levels between the two populations in relative terms.

9 Urban/rural: The 1871 Census defines urban as the population living in incorporated villages, towns, and cities, regardless of size. Rural includes all of the remaining population. The Canadian Historical Mobility Project (Darroch and Ornstein 1984) uses the conventional census definition for urban-rural, but also classifies as urban a few places in the Maritimes where the population density was high in areas surrounding urban centres, that is, the census district. The 1971 Census defines urban as

(1) population of incorporated cities, towns, and villages with a population of 1,000 and over, plus (2) unincorporated places of 1,000 and over having a population density of at least 1,000 per square mile, plus (3) built-up fringes of (1) and (2) having a minimum density of at least 1,000 per square mile. Rural includes all the remaining population.

10 Index of marital assimilation: This variable has been taken as a basic index of social assimilation (Gordon 1964). It is derived from four ethno-religious marital types ranging from marriages where husband and wife are of different ethnicities and different religions to marriages where husband and wife have the same ethnicity and religion. The former is indicative of complete marital assimilation, while the latter indicates no marital assimilation. The index is also dichotomized for utilization as the dependent variable in the logistic regression analysis.

B: INDEXES OF RESIDENTIAL SEGREGATION

TABLE B:1

Indexes of residential segregation for selected ethnic origin populations, Canada, 1871 and 1971

Ethnic origin	1871	1971
British		42.9
English	43.0	–
Irish	40.5	–
Scottish	41.6	–
French	78.5	73.5
German	57.9	41.7
Italian	–	49.1
Dutch	–	38.5
Polish	–	35.0
Scandinavian	–	55.9
Ukrainian	–	47.5
Other	46.3	31.8

SOURCE: *1871 Census of Canada*, Volume 1, Table III; Statistics Canada, *1971 Census of Canada*, Volume Sp-4, Catalogue 92-774, Table 2

NOTE: Dash indicates that data are unavailable or not used in the calculation of Spearman's Rank Order Correlation.

Notes

CHAPTER ONE: INTRODUCTION

1 The original agreements resulted in the admittance of 150 nationals from India, 100 from Pakistan, and 50 from Ceylon, annually. In 1958 the numbers were increased slightly. See Kalbach (1970:21).

2 'Almost immediately (following the removal of restrictions based on ethnic origin) considerable increases in the number of immigrants from China, India, Pakistan, and the West Indies occurred' (Burnet and Palmer 1988:41).

3 A detailed description of the sampling technique used to create the Public Use Sample is presented in Chapter 2, Section 1 under the title Sample Design (Statistics Canada 1975: 2.1.1–2.4.1).

4 The amount of ethnic intermarriage in 1971 suffers from further underestimation due to the presentation of data for Scandinavians, rather than its components of Danish, Swedish, Icelandic, and Norwegian. The usual reason given for not providing data for individual ethnic origin populations is size. Small groups are generally included in Other. Witness the addition of more recent immigrant groups to the publications of the 1981 Census that were previously included in Other in the 1971 Census.

5 It should be noted that the Public Use Sample Tapes are only a sample, and, therefore, the Ns will not necessarily agree with those from census publications. The tape documentation states 'they will inevitably differ to some extent, due to the chance in selection of actual cases for the Public Use Sample' (Statistics Canada 1975: 1.3.1).

6 This suggestion was actually pointed out by Yinger's colleague, Professor John Hewitt. See Yinger (1968:98, n. 6).

7 Goodman (1972) calls it a modified regression approach.

8 Normally the logit is defined as half the log of the odds. Goodman's

convention is that of analysing the log odds, and is followed in this analysis. See Goodman (1972:35).

CHAPTER TWO: INTERMARRIAGE AND ASSIMILATION

1 Gordon refers to this definition as the 'authoritative definition' of acculturation crucial to the field of anthropology. He also points out that 'assimilation' and 'acculturation' are often used to mean the same thing, but that sociologists are more likely to use the former, while anthropologists prefer the latter.

2 Gordon's theory of assimilation is essentially a reformulation of the theory of assimilation based on previous research. He examines the use of the terms 'assimilation' and 'acculturation' and the variables utilized to arrive at the various definitions. His overall aim was to isolate these variables and take another look at the process of assimilation by building on the nomenclature and to suggest relationships between characteristics.

3 In 1921 Drachsler published a monograph entitled *Intermarriage in New York City*. A year earlier he published the 'companion volume' *Democracy and Assimilation*. This volume contained a more 'popular discussion and interpretation of the data' than did the 1921 monograph. See Drachsler's preface (1921) for further elaboration. It should also be noted that Drachsler's data were for individuals living in an urban environment, i.e., New York City.

4 Generation refers to native born and foreign born.

5 The ten groups included Germans, Swedes, Finns, French, Irish, Polish, English, Dutch, Norwegians, and Bohemians.

6 Bugelski indicates that he was not prepared to draw strong conclusions from his investigation because the study was preliminary and was done only for the city of Buffalo and, therefore, was not necessarily representative of the national scene. He also cited the need for more research on the Italians and Poles before his findings could be considered firm rather than tentative.

7 Occupations of grooms were combined to represent three levels, namely, high, middle, and low. High included managerial, professional, administrative, and related occupations. The middle level included clerical, sales, craftsmen, and related occupations. The lowest level included non-household service workers, private household workers, labourers, farmworkers, operatives, and related occupations. See 151-2.

8 Glick further indicates that the selective process between Blacks and Whites is referred to as exchange theory in that Blacks tend to offer more education when they marry a person who is white. See 294.

9 Alba and Golden indicate that the relationship between ethnicity and

religion in their research is weak because data on religion was not actually measured by the survey. In addition, they make it clear that 'individuals identified as Jewish or Catholic in fact contain individuals of other religions.' See Alba and Golden (1986:217).

10 Bernard's data were taken from Federal U.S. Censuses for 1850-80 and from the state of Wisconsin marriage registrations for 1890, 1900, 1910, and 1920. See Chapter 2, n. 14 for more detail.

11 Group factors are defined as characteristics of the group, such as its size, sex ratio, and age composition. Individual factors refer to the characteristics of a person, such as occupation, income, educational level, and generation.

12 The Finns were the largest ethnic group living in Conneaut and represented about 90 per cent of the population.

13 Monahan reveals an interesting story regarding pressures exerted on the Census Bureau not to release the 1957 CPS because it included a question on religion. See Monahan (1971: 85-6) for more details.

14 The authors used Rank Order Correlations. See 330n.

15 They suggest that homogeneity and cohesiveness are inversely related to rates of Catholic intermarriage, and the higher the socio-economic status, the higher the rate of Catholic intermarriage. See 331-3.

16 The 'traditional ethnicities' included Spanish, Italian, Polish, German, East European, Irish, Lithuanian, French Canadian, and English.

17 Hurd's 1941 Census Monograph was published posthumously circa 1964. The original manuscript was discovered by W.E. Kalbach while he was collecting data for his own 1960 Census Monograph. It seems that it had been set aside due to the Government's reluctance to publish it at the time because it apparently felt that the nature of the research constituted a sensitive issue. Kalbach's encouragement to publish it resulted in the publication of a limited edition of the monograph.

18 Hurd notes that limitations of the data were indicated by Niles Carpenter and Dr. Leon Truesdell in their reviews of his 1921 and 1931 monographs, respectively (see 1941 Census Monograph, 97, nn. 39, 40). Carpenter noted that the use of such data ignored marriages that were infertile and moreover, that it was probable that ethnically endogamous marriages were more fertile than exogamous marriages. It was recognized that this would have the effect of underestimating exogamy and overestimating endogamy. Truesdell suggested that ethnic groups were likely to be differentially represented in the data, in that the statistics would favour the older more established groups compared to the more recent arrivals.

19 Kalbach calculated propensities as the ratio of actual marriages to expected marriages.

20 Data were not actually selected for every year, but for every five years,

i.e., 1922, 1927, 1932, etc.

21 Data were unavailable for Canada as a whole in 1922. See Table 2, 257.

CHAPTER THREE: CANADA'S IMMIGRANTS

1 The census definition for ethnic origin is used throughout this analysis. In 1871 individuals were asked what their origin was (see 1871 Census, Volume I, p. xxii–xxiv). Kralt suggests that 'the intention of the question on origin was to create a sharp distinction between origin and citizenship or nationality.' He uses the phrase racial origin when referring to the 1871 variable (1980:19). Ethnic origin refers to the ethnic or cultural background traced through the father's side in 1971.

2 Simple percentage distribution maps cannot directly show the extent to which a population may be over- or underconcentrated in a particular area. The index of relative concentration used in the 1871 and 1971 maps permits a direct interpretation. An index of 100.0 means that its percentage of the census district population was identical to its percentage in Canada as a whole, and it was neither under- nor overrepresented in that particular district. An index of 110.0 means that the population is overrepresented by 10 per cent, while an index of 70.0 indicates an underrepresentation of 30 per cent.

CHAPTER FOUR: CANADA'S ETHNIC POPULATION

1 In 1871 enumerators were asked to record the ethnic origin of people. The question was intended to make clear distinctions between origin, citizenship, and nationality (Kralt 1980). The 1971 Census asked individuals to indicate 'the ethnic or cultural group that he or his ancestor (on the male side) belonged on coming to this continent.' Earlier censuses asked the same basic question. While data collection procedures have changed over the years from personal enumeration to self-enumeration, it is impossible to determine the precise effect it would have on the quality of the data.

2 According to the 1971 Census of Canada, 44.6 per cent of the population was British in origin, 28.6 per cent was French, and 26.7 per cent was of the other cultural or ethnic origins (Statistics Canada, *1971 Census of Canada*, Special Tabulations).

3 Alba and Golden (1986:217) acknowledge the potentially important influence of religion on tendencies for ethnic intermarriage. Since no large-scale data set containing ancestry and religion exists in the United States, they were only able to report that ethnic intermarriage appeared weaker in their analysis than it would have been had they been able to consider the effects of both variables.

4 Data for English, Irish, and Scottish are available as special tabulations from Statistics Canada, but the costs were prohibitive.

5 As previously noted, the Presbyterians, Methodists, and Congregationalists merged in 1925 to form the United Church of Canada. Since then the censuses have reported United Church. Not all Presbyterians joined the Union of 1925. The numbers were substantial enough to warrant a separate category.

6 These percentages are not the same as those calculated directly from the 1871 Census. Farmers, for example, comprised 55 per cent of the labour force if the published figures were used. The data reported here are taken from the Canadian Historical Mobility Project, which drew a sample of over 10,000 households from the original data base. Because of the nature of the sample the figures vary from those from published sources, but the patterns and rank order are the same.

7 'Other' includes the more recent immigrant groups such as the Chinese and East Indians, most of whom had high levels of educational attainment.

8 Illiteracy is measured by the proportion of those with less than a grade five level of completed schooling in 1971. While this may overestimate the degree of illiteracy, it was selected on the basis of the researcher's experience as an elementary school teacher during the 1960s. Grades one through four were, and still are, considered primary school and is the period of time during which all of the skills necessary for reading and writing simple messages are taught. If, for example, reading was taught using phonics, as it was during the sixties, a child would not learn all of the skills for reading until the end of the fourth grade. From the fifth grade on students concentrated on sentence structure and construction rather than on the rudiments of reading. It is assumed that a person who could read could also write if he completed his primary education. It is also recognized that immigrants may have come from a different educational system than Canada's, in which case completion of grade levels by Canadian standards may not accurately measure their level of literacy. While the measure of literacy used for 1971 is not truly comparable to that for 1871, it is the best division of level of education given the form of the data available from the 1971 Public Use Sample. It at least illustrates an important difference in educational levels between the two populations in relative terms.

CHAPTER FIVE:
PREVALENCE AND PATTERNS OF INTERMARRIAGE

1 The Ns for the native born range from a high of 38 for English Anglicans to a low of 5 for German Lutheran husbands. They range from a high of

59 for foreign-born English Anglicans to a low of 2 for French Catholic husbands. In all, 115 native-born and 123 foreign-born husbands outmarried.

2 Kornacker indicates that late nineteenth century U.S. immigrants 'characterized intermarriage as a crossing of lines of national origin' and that 'first American-born white Americans considered religion rather than national origins as the crucial mate selection boundary' (1971:155).

CHAPTER SIX: GROUP AND INDIVIDUAL FACTORS

1 Indexes of residential segregation were calculated using census districts as the geographic unit in 1871 and census divisions in 1971. See Chapter 3 for a discussion of the index. It should be noted that index of dissimilarity and index of segregation in this research are the same. The terms are used synonymously.

CHAPTER SEVEN: CONCLUSION

1 An example of the categories provided is British, French, and Other. Special tabulations could be requested showing the individual origins reported by each respondent in the Canadian population. In the last few years, however, Statistics Canada has instituted a cost recovery policy. Under such conditions it is unlikely that a replication of Lieberson's analysis using Canadian data could be afforded. Kalbach and Richard (1985) conducted an exploratory analysis of the relationships between the nativity of family heads, types of ethnically mixed husband-wife families, and selected indexes of assimilation and socio-economic integration for the Toronto CMA, 1981. It was determined that the analysis did not shed new light on what is known about the advantages of being native born versus being an immigrant. It did, however, demonstrate what could be done with information not previously provided by earlier Canadian censuses by perhaps revealing something new or by reminding one of something long forgotten regarding the importance of ethnic mixing in a multi-ethnic society dominated by one or two large and culturally distinct populations. It also suggested that ethnic mixing based on the multiple origin response to the 1981 Census question on ethnicity may be an underestimate of the actual amount that has occurred over time. If this is the case it may also be that researchers have underestimated the socio-economic and cultural significance of ethnic mixing for Canadian society. The data for this analysis were derived from the 1981 Public Use Sample.

APPENDIX A: VARIABLES

1 As previously noted, the 1971 Census 1 per cent Public Use Sample does not provide data for Prince Edward Island and the Territories because they do not meet the minimum size required for inclusion in the sample. This action was taken by Statistics Canada in the interests of preserving confidentiality.

2 Lieberson and Waters (1985) utilize these two age cohorts in their analysis of marriage patterns among individuals of mixed ethnic origins. They point out that 'because information on marriages obtained from the census are basically prevalence data rather than incidence data,' all one can really examine at any age is the 'ethnic combinations of the survivors of such marriages' (ibid.: 44). Moreover, these data do not indicate when a couple were married, nor do they reveal who got married and are now divorced or reveal situations where one of the spouses is deceased. They also acknowledge that it is possible for persons in the older cohort to have just been married for the first time and, therefore, more recently than a 24-year-old woman who was married for the first time at age 16. They go on to indicate that 'it is not unduly bold to compare the age cohorts as a rough way of describing the shifts in out-marriage for groups with a sharp drop-off between the youngest and oldest cohorts' (ibid.: 45).

Bibliography

Abramson, Harold J.

  1973 *Ethnic Diversity in Catholic America*. New York: Wiley

Akenson, Donald H.

  1984 *The Irish in Ontario*. Kingston and Montreal: McGill-Queen's University Press

Alba, Richard D.

  1987 'Interpreting the Parameters of Log-Linear Models.' *Sociological Methods & Research* 16:45-77

  1976 'Social Assimilation among American Catholic National Origin Groups.' *American Sociological Review* 41:1030-46

Alba, Richard D., and Reid M. Golden

  1986 'Patterns of Ethnic Intermarriage in the United States.' *Social Forces* 65:202-23

Avery, Donald

  1979 *Dangerous Foreigners*. Toronto: McClelland & Stewart

Avery, D.H., and J.K. Fedorowicz

  1982 *The Poles in Canada*. Ottawa: Canadian Historical Association

Balakrishnan, T.R.

  1976 'Ethnic Residential Segregation in the Metropolitan Area of Canada.' *Canadian Journal of Sociology* 77:491-510

Barron, Milton M.

  1946 *People Who Intermarry*. Syracuse, NY: Syracuse University Press

  1951 'Research on Intermarriage: A Survey of Accomplishments and Prospects.' *American Journal of Sociology* 57:249-55

  1972 'Intergroup Aspects of Choosing a Mate.' In M. Barron (ed.), *The Blending American: Patterns of Intermarriage*. Chicago: Quadrangle Books, 36-48

Barton, Joseph
  1975 *Peasants and Strangers*. Cambridge, MA: Harvard University Press
Belkin, Simon
  1966 *Through Narrow Gates*. Montreal: The Canadian Jewish Congress and
  the Jewish Colonization Association
Bender, Eugene I., and George Kagiwada
  1968 'Hansen's Law of "Third Generation Return" and the Study of
  American Religio-Ethnic Groups.' *Phylon* 29:360–70
Berkson, Joseph
  1944 'Application of the Logistic Function to Bio-Assay.' *Journal of the
  American Statistical Association* 39:357–65
  1953 'A Statistically Precise and Relatively Simple Method of Estimating
  the Bio-Assay with Quantal Response, Based on Logistic Function.'
  Journal of the American Statistical Association 48:565–99
Bernard, Richard M.
  1976 'Intermarriage Patterns Among Immigrants and Natives in Wiscon-
  sin, 1850–1920: The Effects of Generation, Group Sizes and Sex
  Ratios.' Paper presented to the Ninth Annual Conference on Social-
  Political History, New York
  1980 *The Melting Pot and the Altar*. Minneapolis: University of Minnesota
  Press
Berry, John W., Rudolf Kalin, and Donald M. Taylor
  1977 *Multiculturalism and Ethnic Attitudes in Canada*. Ottawa: Minister of
  Supply and Services
Besanceney, Paul H.
  1965 'On Reporting Rates of Intermarriage.' *American Journal of Sociology*
  70: 717–21
Blau, Peter M.
  1977 *Inequality and Heterogeneity*. New York: Free Press
Blau, Peter M., Terry C. Blum, and Joseph E. Schwartz
  1982 'Heterogeneity and Intermarriage.' *American Sociological Review*
  47:45–62
Boissevain, Jeremy
  1970 *The Italians of Montreal: Social Adjustment in a Plural Society*. Ottawa:
  Information Canada
Bossard, James
  1939 'Nationality and Nativity as Factors in Marriage.' *American Sociological Review* 4:792–8
Boyd, Monica, John Goyder, Frank Jones, Hugh McRoberts, Peter Pineo, and
  John Porter
  1985 *Ascription and Achievement: Studies in Mobility and Status Attainment in
  Canada*. Ottawa: Carleton University Press

Brownfield, David, and Eric W. Carlson
   1983 'Minimum Logit Chi-Square Regression: A Useful Statistical Proce-
        dure for Evaluation Research.' Unpublished paper. Department of
        Sociology, University of Arizona
Bugelski, B.R.
   1961 'Assimilation through Intermarriage.' *Social Forces* 40:148-53
Bumpass, Larry
   1970 'The Trend of Interfaith Marriages in the United States.' *Social Biol-
        ogy* 17:253-9
Bumstead, J.M.
   1982 *The Scots in Canada*. Ottawa: Canadian Historical Association
Burgess, Ernest W., and Paul Wallin
   1943 'Homogamy in Social Characteristics.' *American Journal of Sociology*
        49:109-24
Burma, John H.
   1963 'Interethnic Marriage in Los Angeles, 1948-1959.' *Social Forces*
        42:156-165
Burnet, Jean
   1972 *Ethnic Groups in Upper Canada*. Ontario Historical Society Research
        Publication no. 1
   1976 'Ethnicity: Canadian Experience and Policy.' *Sociological Focus*
        9:199-207
   1987 'Multiculturalism in Canada.' In L. Dreidger (ed.), *Ethnic Canada*.
        Toronto: Copp Clark Pitman, 65-79
Burnet, Jean R., and Howard Palmer
   1988 *'Coming Canadians.'* Toronto: McClelland & Stewart
Campbell, Douglas F., and David C. Neice
   1979 *Ties That Bind: Structure and Marriage in Nova Scotia*. Port Credit, ON:
        Scribbler's Press
Carisse, C.
   1975 'Cultural Orientations in Marriages Between French and English
        Canadians.' In S. Parvez Wakil (ed.), *Marriage, Family and Society*. Scar-
        borough: Butterworth (Canada), 97-112
Carpenter, Niles
   1927 *Immigrants and Their Children 1920: A Study Based on Census Statistics
        Relative to the Foreign-Born and the Native White of Foreign or Mixed Parent-
        age*. Washington: Census Monograph VII
Cohen, Steven Martin
   1980 *Interethnic Marriage and Friendship*. New York: Arno Press
Darroch, Gordon
   1986 'Class, Land and Families in Nineteenth Century Canada: A Discus-
        sion of Relevance and Methods in Social History.' Paper presented at
        the Canadian Population Association Annual Meeting, Winnipeg

Darroch, A. Gordon, and Wilfred G. Marston
  1969 'Ethnic Differentiation: Ecological Aspects of a Multidimensional Concept.' *The International Migration Review* 4:71-95
Darroch, Gordon, and Michael Ornstein
  1980 'Ethnicity and Occupation Structure in Canada in 1871: The Vertical Mosaic in Historical Perspective.' *Canadian Historical Review* 61:305-33
  1984 'Family and Household in Nineteenth Century Canada: Regional Patterns and Regional Economies.' *Journal of Family History* 9:158-77
  1985 'Ethnicity and Class: Transitions over a Decade, Ontario 1861-1871.' *Canadian Historical Association Historical Papers* Spring: 111-37
Dawson, C.A.
  1936 *Group Settlement*. Toronto: Macmillan
Department of Agriculture
  1882 *Census of Canada, 1880-81*. Volume I Ottawa: MacLean, Roger & Co.
Department of the Secretary of State of Canada
  1979 *The Canadian Family Tree*. Ottawa: Minister of Supply and Services
  1987 *Multiculturalism ... being Canadian*. Ottawa: Minister of Supply and Services
Drachsler, Julius
  1920 *Democracy and Assimilation: The Blending of American Heritages in America*. New York: Macmillan
  1921 *Intermarriage in New York City*. New York: Columbia University Press
Duncan, O.D.
  1975 'Minimum Logit Chi-Square Regression Using SPSS.' Unpublished report. University of Arizona
Feinberg, Stephen E.
  1980 *The Analysis of Cross-Classified Categorical Data*. 2nd ed. Cambridge, MA: MIT Press
Fitzpatrick, Joseph P.
  1966 'Intermarriage of Puerto Ricans in New York City.' *American Journal of Sociology* 71:395-406
Frideres, J., J. Goldstein, and R. Gilbert
  1971 'The Impact of Jewish-Gentile Intermarriage in Canada: An Alternative View.' *Journal of Comparative Family Studies* 11:268-75
Gerus, O.W., and J.E. Rea
  1985 *The Ukrainians in Canada*. Ottawa: Canadian Historical Association
Gibbon, John Murray
  1938 *Canadian Mosaic*. Toronto: McClelland & Stewart
Glazer, Nathan, and Daniel Patrick Moynihan
  1963 *Beyond the Melting Pot*. Cambridge, MA: MIT Press
Glenn, Norval D.
  1982 'Interreligious Marriage in the United States: Patterns and Recent Trends.' *Journal of Marriage and the Family* 44:555-66

Glick, Paul C.
1960 'Intermarriage and Fertility Patterns Among Persons in Major Religious Groups.' *Eugenics Quarterly* 7:31-8
1970 'Intermarriage among Ethnic Groups in the United States.' *Social Biology* 17:292-8
Goodman, L.A.
1972 'A Modified Multiple Regression Approach to the Analysis of Dichotomous Variables.' *American Sociological Review* 37:28-46
1975 'The Relationship Between Modified and Usual Multiple-Regression Approaches to the Analysis of Dichotomous Variables.' In David Heise (ed.), *Sociological Methodology 1976*. San Francisco: Jossey-Bass
Gordon, Milton M.
1964 *Assimilation in American Life*. New York: Oxford University Press
Greeley, Andrew M.
1970 'Religious Intermarriage in a Denominational Society.' *American Journal of Sociology* 75:949-52
1971 *Why Can't They Be Like Us?* New York: E.P. Dutton
Griffiths, Naomi
1973 *The Acadians: Creation of a People*. Toronto: McGraw-Hill Ryerson
Hagood, Margaret Jarman
1951 *Statistics for Sociologists*. New York: Henry Holt
Hanushek, Eric A., and John E. Jackson
1977 *Statistical Methods for Social Scientists*. New York: Academic Press
Harris, R. Cole, and John Warkentin
1974 *Canada before Confederation*. Toronto: Oxford University Press
Hawkins, Freda
1988 *Canada and Immigration*. 2nd. ed. Kingston and Montreal: McGill-Queen's University Press
Heer, David M.
1962 'The Trend of Interfaith Marriages in Canada, 1922-1957.' *American Sociological Review* 27:245-50
Heer, David M., and Charles A. Hubay, Jr.
1975 'The Trend of Interfaith Marriages in Canada: 1922 to 1972.' In S. Parvez Wakil (ed.), *Marriage, Family and Society*. Scarborough: Butterworth, 85-96
Herberg, Will
1955 *Protestant, Catholic, Jew*. New York: Doubleday
Hirschman, C.
1983 'America's Melting Pot Reconsidered.' *Annual Review of Sociology* 9:397-423
Hobart, Charles W.
1975 'Changing Family Patterns Among Ukrainian Canadians in Alberta.' In S. Parvez Wakil (ed.), *Marriage, Family and Society*. Scarborough:

Butterworth, 401–15

Hollingshead, A.B.

1950 'Cultural Factors in the Selection of Marriage Mates.' *American Sociological Review* 15:619–27

Hurd, Burton W.

1929 *Origin, Birthplace, Nationality and Language of the Canadian People*. 1921 Census Monograph, Dominion Bureau of Statistics. Ottawa: King's Printer

1942 *Racial Origins and Nativity of the Canadian People*. 1931 Census Monograph, Dominion Bureau of Statistics. Ottawa: King's Printer

1964 *Ethnic Origin and Nativity of the Canadian People*. 1941 Census Monograph, Dominion Bureau of Statistics. Ottawa: Queen's Printer

Jansen, Clifford

1982 'Inter-Ethnic Marriages.' *International Journal of Comparative Sociology* 23:225–35

Jiobu, Robert M.

1988 *Ethnicity and Assimilation*. Albany: State University of New York Press

Johnson, H.B.

1946 'Intermarriage between German Pioneers and Other Nationalities in Minnesota in 1860 and 1870.' *American Journal of Sociology* 51:299–304

Johnson, Robert

1980 *Religious Assortative Marriage in the United States*. New York: Academic Press

Kalbach, Warren E.

1970 *The Impact of Immigration on Canada's Population*. Ottawa: Information Canada

1974 *The Effect of Immigration on Canada's Population*. Ottawa: Information Canada

1975 'The Demography of Marriage.' In S. Parvez Wakil (ed.), *Marriage, Family and Society* Scarborough: Butterworth, 59–84

1981 *Ethnic Residential Segregation and Its Significance for the Individual in an Urban Setting*. Research Paper no. 124. Toronto: Centre for Urban and Community Studies

1983 'Propensities for Intermarriage in Canada, as Reflected in the Ethnic Origins of Husbands and Their Wives: 1961–1971.' In K. Ishwaran (ed.), *Marriage and Divorce in Canada*. Toronto: Methuen, 196–212

Kalbach, Warren E., and Wayne W. McVey

1979 *The Demographic Bases of Canadian Society*. Toronto: McGraw-Hill Ryerson

Kalbach W.E., and M.A. Richard

1985a 'Ethnic Connectedness: How Binding Is the Tie?' In *Central and East European Ethnicity in Canada: Adaptation and Preservation*. Edmonton, AB: Central and East European Studies Society of Alberta, 99–109

1985b 'Multiple Origins and Ethnic Exogamy: Clues to Assimilation and Socioeconomic Integration of Families in the 1981 Census of Canada.' Paper presented at the Annual Meeting of the Canadian Sociology and Anthropology Association Learned Societies University of Montreal

1988a 'Alternative Mobility Patterns for Canadian Immigrants: The Ethnic Church, Canadian Church and No Church.' Paper presented to the Population Association of America Annual Meeting New Orleans, LA, April

1988b 'Ethnic-Religious Identity, Acculturation, and Social and Economic Achievement of Canada's Post-War Minority Populations.' Report prepared for the Review of Demography and Its Implications for Economic and Social Policy, Health and Welfare Canada, October

Kallen, Evelyn
1976 'Family Life Styles and Jewish Culture.' In K. Ishwaran (ed.), *The Canadian Family*. Rev. ed. Toronto: Holt, Rinehart and Winston, 41–5

1977 *Spanning the Generations: A Study in Jewish Identity*. Don Mills, ON: Longman

Katz, M.B., M.J. Doucet, and Mark J. Stern
1982 *The Social Organization of Early Industrial Capitalism*. Cambridge, MA/ London, Eng: Harvard University Press

Kennedy, Ruby Jo Reeves
1944 'Single or Triple Melting Pot?: Intermarriage Trends in New Haven, 1870–1940.' *American Journal of Sociology* 49:331–9

1952 'Single or Triple Melting Pot? Intermarriage in New Haven, 1870–1950.' *American Journal of Sociology* 58:56–66

Knoke, David
1975 'A Comparison of Log-Linear and Regression Models for Systems of Dichotomous Variables.' *Sociological Methods and Research* 3:416–34

Knoke, David, and Peter J. Burke
1980 *Log-Linear Models*. Beverly Hills, CA: Sage

Kolehmainen, John
1936 'A Study of Marriage in a Finnish Community.' *American Journal of Sociology* 42:317–82

Kornacker, Mildred
1971 'Cultural Significance of Intermarriage: A Comparative Approach.' *International Journal of the Sociology of the Family*. Special Issue, 147–56

Kralt, John M.
1980 'Ethnic Origin in the Canadian Census 1871–1981.' In W.R. Petryshyn (ed.) *Changing Realities: Social Trends among Ukrainian Canadians*. Edmonton: Canadian Institute of Ukrainian Studies, 18–49

LaPiere, Richard T., and Paul R. Farnsworth
1942 *Social Psychology*. 2nd ed. New York: McGraw-Hill

Leacy, F.H. (ed.)

    1983 *Historical Statistics of Canada*. 2nd ed. Ottawa: Statistics Canada.

Lehmann, Heinz

    1986 *German Canadians 1750-1937*. St. John's, NF: Jesperson Press

Lieberson, Stanley

    1963 *Ethnic Patterns in American Cities*. New York: The Free Press of Glencoe

Lieberson, Stanley, and Mary Waters

    1985 'Recent Social Trends, Ethnic Mixtures in the United States.' *Sociology and Social Research* 70:43–52

Locke, Harvey J., Georges Sabagh, and Mary Margaret Thomas

    1957 'Interfaith Marriages.' *Social Forces* 4:329–33

Makowski, W.B.

    1967 *History and Integration of Poles in Canada*. Niagara Peninsula: Canadian Polish Congress

Mannion, John J.

    1974 *Irish Settlements in Eastern Canada*. University of Toronto, Geography Department, Research Publication no. 12

Manpower and Immigration

    1974a *The Immigration Program*. Ottawa: Information Canada

    1974b *Immigration and Population Statistics*. Ottawa: Information Canada

Marcson, Simon

    1950 'A Theory of Intermarriage and Assimilation.' *Social Forces* 29:75–8

McLaughlin, K.M.

    1985 *The Germans in Canada*. Ottawa: Canadian Historical Association

Merton, Robert K.

    1972 'Intermarriage and the Social Structure: Facts and Theory.' In M. Barron (ed.), *The Blending American: Patterns of Intermarriage*. Chicago: Quadrangle 12–35

Miner, Horace

    1939 *St. Denis*. Toronto: University of Toronto Press

Mittlebach, Frank G., and Joan W. Moore

    1968 'Ethnic Endogamy: The Case of Mexican Americans.' *American Journal of Sociology* 74:50–62

Monahan, Thomas P.

    1971 'The Extent of Interdenominational Marriage in the United States.' *Journal for the Scientific Study of Religion* 10:85–107

Morton, Desmond

    1983 *A Short History of Canada*. Edmonton: Hurtig

Nelson, Lowry

    1943 'Intermarriage Among Nationality Groups in a Rural Area of Minnesota.' *American Journal of Sociology* 48:585–92

Nett, Emily

    1981 'Canadian Families in Social-Historical Perspective.' *Canadian Journal of Sociology* 6:239-60

Ontario
1979 *Ontario Ethnocultural Profiles*. Ministry of Culture and Recreation

Pagnini, Deanna
1988 'Intermarriage and Social Distance Among U.S. Immigrants at the Turn of the Century.' Paper presented at the Population Association of America Annual Meeting, New Orleans, LA, April

Palmer, Howard
1972 *Land of the Second Chance*. Lethbridge, AB: The Lethbridge Herald
1975 *Immigration and the Rise of Multiculturalism*. Toronto: Copp Clark

Park, Robert E.
1930 'Assimilation, Social.' In *Encyclopedia of the Social Sciences*, Vol. 2, Edwin Seligman and Alvin Johnson (eds.). New York: Macmillan

Park, Robert E., and Ernest W. Burgess
1921 *Introduction to the Science of Sociology*. Chicago: University of Chicago Press

Pineo, Peter C.
1987 'The Social Standing of Ethnic and Racial Groupings.' In L. Driedger (ed.), *Ethnic Canada* Toronto: Copp Clark Pitman, 256-72

Porter, John
1965 *The Vertical Mosaic*. Toronto: University of Toronto Press

Price, C.A., and J. Zubrzycki
1962 'Immigrant Marriage Patterns in Australia.' *Population Studies* 16:123-33

Radecki, Henry, and Benedykt Heydenkorn
1976 *A Member of a Distinguished Family*. Toronto: McClelland & Stewart

Ramu, G.N.
1976 'The Family and Marriage in Canada.' In G.N. Ramu and Stuart D. Johnson (eds.), *Introduction to Canadian Society*. Toronto: Macmillan, 295-348

Reitz, Jeffrey G.
1980 *The Survival of Ethnic Groups*. Toronto: McGraw-Hill Ryerson

Reynolds, Lloyd George
1935 *The British Immigrant*. Toronto: Oxford University Press

Richmond, A.H., and W.E. Kalbach
1980 *Factors in the Adjustment of Immigrants and Their Descendants*. Ottawa: Statistics Canada

Rodman, Hyman
1965 'Technical Note on Two Rates of Intermarriage.' *American Sociological Review* 30:776-8

Rogoff, Natalie
1953 *Recent Trends in Occupational Mobility*. Glencoe, IL: Free Press

Ryder, Norman B.

1955 'The Interpretation of Origin Statistics.' *Canadian Journal of Economics and Political Science* 21:466-79

Schoen, Robert, and Lawrence E. Cohen
  1980 'Ethnic Endogamy Among Mexican American Grooms: A Reanalysis of Generational and Occupational Effects.' *Amercian Journal of Sociology* 86:359-66

Sills, David L. (ed.)
  1968 *International Encyclopedia of the Social Sciences.* New York: Macmillan Company and The Free Press 9:412-15

Smith, W.G.
  1920 *A Study in Canadian Immigration.* Toronto: Ryerson Press
  1922 *Building the Nation.* Toronto: Ryerson Press

Snedcor, George W., and William G. Cochran
  1967 *Statistical Methods.* 6th ed. Ames, IA: Iowa State University Press

Sorenson, Ann Marie
  1988 'The Fertility and Language Characteristics of Mexican-American and Non-Hispanic Husbands and Wives.' *The Sociological Quarterly* 29:111-30

SPSS Inc.
  1986 *SPSSX User's Guide.* 2nd ed. Chicago: SPSS

Statistics Canada
  1972 *Dictionary of the 1971 Census Terms.* Ottawa: Minister of Industry, Trade and Commerce
  1974 *Vital Statistics 1971.* Ottawa: Information Canada, Volume 2: Table 14
  1975 *Public Use Sample Tapes, User Documentation, 1971 Census of Canada.* Ottawa: Minister of Industry, Trade and Commerce

Stevens Gillian, and Gray Swicegood
  1987 'The Linguistic Context of Ethnic Endogamy.' *American Sociological Review* 52:73-82

Stevens, James
  1986 *Applied Multivariate Statistics for the Social Sciences.* New Jersey: Lawrence Erlbaum Associates Publishers

Synge, Jane
  1976 'The Sociology of Canadian Education.' In Ramu and Johnson (eds.), *Introduction to Canadian Society.* Toronto: Macmillan, 401-36

Theil, Henri
  1970 'On the Estimation of Relationships Involving Qualitative Variables.' *American Journal of Sociology* 76:103-54

Thomas, John L.
  1951 'The Factor of Religion in the Selection of Marriage Mates.' *American Sociological Review* 16:487-91

Travis, Paul
  1973 'Religious Intermarriage and Intermarriages in Canada 1934-1969: A

Methodological and Empirical Investigation.' MS thesis, University of Wisconsin

United Nations
1965 *Demographic Yearbook, 1964*. New York: Statistical Office of the United Nations, Table 33: 690

Urquhart, M.C., and K. Buckley
1965 *Historical Statistics of Canada*. Toronto: Macmillan

Veevers, J. E.
1977 *The Family in Canada*. A profile study from the 1971 Census of Canada. Volume V- Part 3, Bulletin 5.3-3. Ottawa: Statistics Canada

Wade, Mason
1968 *The French Canadians 1760-1967*. Rev. ed. Vol. 1. Toronto: Macmillan

Woodsworth, James S.
1909 *Strangers Within Our Gates, or Coming Canadians*. 2nd. ed. Toronto: Young People's Movement Department of the Methodist Church of Canada

Yinger, Milton J.
1968 'Research Note on Interfaith Marriage Statistics.' *Journal for the Scientific Study of Religion* 7:97-107
1985 'Ethnicity.' *Annual Review of Sociology* 11:151-80

Zangwill, I.
1909 *The Melting Pot*. New York: Macmillan

Name Index

Subject Index

Acculturation: defined as, 17, 162; exogamy and, 28
Age, definition of, 158
Age and sex composition, 89-90, 92; ethnic populations and, 93-6
Anglo-conformity, 18-19
Assimilation: and convergence hypothesis, 17; intermarriage and, 19-33; Gordon's theory of, 18, 20, 39, 114-15, 119-20, 124, 146, 153, 162; pathways to, 120; and progress through intermarriage, 35; religion and, 30; theories of, 17-19

British: and patterns of intermarriage, 110-11, 113; per cent illiterate of, 103; population growth of, 77-9; religious composition of, 82-3

Classical immigration theory, 145
Cultural pluralism, 18-19

Dutch: age and sex composition of, 91, 95-6; immigration patterns of, 60, 62; index of dissimilarity for, 72, 74; intermarriage patterns of, 110, 113-14; nativity distribution of, 81; occupational distribution of, 101-2; per cent illiterate of, 103; population growth of, 78-9; religious affiliation (composition) by nativity of, 87; religious composition of, 83-4; rural-urban distribution of, 96-7; settlement patterns of, 60-2; sex ratios of, 90

Education. *See* Literacy
Educational attainment. *See* Literacy
Emigration, and population growth, 41
English: age and sex composition of, 91, 93-4; immigration patterns of, 48-51; intermarriage patterns of, 108-10, 112-13; nativity distribution of, 81; natural increase importance for, 80; occupational distribution of, 98, 100; per cent illiterate of, 103; population growth of, 48, 77-9; religious affiliation (composition) by nativity of, 84-7; religious composition of, 82-3; rural-urban distribution of, 97; settlement patterns of, 50; sex ratios of, 90

76, 89; of ethnic groups, 90-1; and influence on intermarriage, 111–12
Spearman's rank order correlation (Rho), definition of, 127

Ukrainians: age and sex composition of, 95-6; immigration patterns of, 70, 72; indexes of relative concentration for, 53; intermarriage patterns of, 110, 113; nativity distribution of, 81; occupa-tional distribution of, 101; per cent illiterate of, 103; population growth of, 78-9; religious affiliation (composition) by nativity of, 87-9; religious composition of, 83; rural-urban distribution of, 96-8; settlement patterns of, 70, 73; sex ratios of, 90
United Empire Loyalists, 48-9, 53, 60
Urban-rural, definition of, 158 9